Emily Brontë Criticism

1900–1968

An Annotated Check List

Emily Brontë Criticism
1900-1968

An Annotated Check List

JANET M. BARCLAY

The New York Public Library
Astor, Lenox and Tilden Foundations
&
Readex Books
A Division of Readex Microprint Corporation

ON THE COVER: Emily Brontë's manuscript poems, 1838
Berg Collection of English and American Literature

When days of Beauty deck the earth
Or stormy nights descend,
How well my spirit knows the path
On which it ought to wend.

It seeks the consecrated spot
Beloved in childhood's years,
The space between is all forgot
Its sufferings and its tears.

For transcriptions of the other poems, see C. W. Hatfield's edition of *The Complete Poems of Emily Jane Brontë* (entry A80), poems 88–89.

Copyright © 1974 The New York Public Library
Astor, Lenox and Tilden Foundations

Library of Congress Catalog Card Number: 74–76459
International Standard Book Number: 0–87104–227–4

Distributed by Readex Books

Contents

INTRODUCTION

CRITICISM of Emily Brontë's novel, *Wuthering Heights*, and of her poetry ranges from perceptive literary analysis to sentimental, maudlin interpretation of her work biased by the critic's view of her life story, the historical or the legendary. Because relatively few facts are known about her personal life, the would-be critic or biographer enjoys a wide field for speculation about what might have been. Fortunately, a number of critics choose to contend mainly with the mystery of the meaning of her work, and many biographers painstakingly attempt to separate fact from legend.

The textual history of Emily Brontë's work and especially her poetry is as complex as the history of the biography and criticism. A definitive edition of her poems did not exist until 1941, either because they were not available for publication, or because they were confused with other Brontë poems. Moreover, Charlotte Brontë, in editing the poems for publication after Emily's death, "improved" them. The Gondal story, a literary theory now accepted by many critics as the central framework for some of Emily Brontë's poetry, did not begin to be worked out by scholars until 1923. Perplexing as the poems have been, we do have manuscripts of them; we have none of *Wuthering Heights*. Nevertheless, modern textual bibliography produced an authoritative edition of *Wuthering Heights* in 1963, based on the 1847 first edition.

Wuthering Heights, into the early 1900s often judged an amateurish, ill-constructed novel, was not nearly so widely read as Charlotte Brontë's novels. However, in 1926, C. P. Sanger discovered the intricate genealogical construction of the novel, and pointed out that the plot accurately concurs with English inheritance law. At about the same time, other critics began to look at the novel anew. Gradually *Wuthering Heights* was recognized as a work of art because of the simplicity of the poetic language, the balanced themes and unifying imagery, and the subtly effective double narrative.

The diversity of interpretation of Emily Brontë's work is almost overwhelming, but much of the criticism falls into a pattern if it is seen in the light of the various critical approaches to literature practiced in the twentieth century. In the early part of the century Impressionism was prevalent; the critic simply recorded his personal response to a work. Thus, in 1913, George Saintsbury dismissed *Wuthering Heights* as "an ornament in novel history." Genetic scholarship — overlapping Impressionism — searched for literary sources for a given work: Byron is one choice as a source for Emily Brontë's poems, and Scott and Shakespeare are frequently-mentioned sources for

Wuthering Heights, as in Florence S. Dry's *The Sources of Wuthering Heights* (1937).

Some of the most valuable criticism has been engendered by the literary approach of the New Criticism, which began in the 1940s. A literary work must, according to this school, be closely read and then judged solely as a work of art. The very aspects of *Wuthering Heights* deplored by the earlier critics — the cruelty depicted in the novel, and the double narrative — were discovered by the New Critics to be ingeniously contributory to its art. Mark Schorer (evaluating the metaphors, epithets, and verbs in *Wuthering Heights* in 1949) concluded that it was no cruel tragedy, but a "moral teething" for both Heathcliff and Emily Brontë. Benjamin H. Lehman in 1955 and Carl Woodring in 1957 applauded the double narrative.

Other recent approaches to literature appear in criticism of Emily Brontë. The most startling conclusions are drawn by those who use the psychoanalytical approach; they base their findings both on her writings and on evidence in her biography, or merely on their own conjecture. The social and economic approach to literature brought forth little criticism because of the nature of Emily Brontë's work and her isolation from significant social and economic forces. Nevertheless, Martin Turnell in 1940 wrote an astute analysis in which *Wuthering Heights* is seen as "an indictment of contemporary civilization." Myth-and-symbol interpretation applies readily to Emily Brontë's work: Dorothy Van Ghent's explication of the Window Figure and the Two-children Figure in the novel (1952) is credible, and well-supported by instances in the text of *Wuthering Heights*. An example of the more recent structural linguistics approach is Jeremy Cott's analysis of the last sentence in *Wuthering Heights* (1964), a study adding to an understanding of the poetic art in the novel.

Although Emily Brontë is an eminent author, few attempts have been made to compile extensive and annotated check lists of items about her. To date, one of the best — though it includes Charlotte Brontë and is not annotated — is Joseph Henry Dugas' bibliography for his "The Literary Reputation of the Brontës: 1846–1951" [a dissertation] (1951). *The Four Brontës* by Lawrence and E. M. Hanson (1949) contains a ten-page bibliography to which the same limitations apply. Edward G. Wagenknecht [*Cavalcade of the English Novel* (1943)] adds a supplementary bibliography in his 1954 edition, and Mary Visick's *The Genesis of Wuthering Heights* (1958) contains a selected annotated bibliography. Mildred G. Christian's chapter in *Victorian Fiction: A Guide to Research* (1964) is a selected bibliography in chronological form, and confines itself to the preceding thirty years of work on Emily Brontë. Other than these, there are only the four- and five-page bibliographies printed at the end of various works on Emily Brontë.

Literary criticism of Emily Brontë in the nineteenth century has specialized value; it is, however, in the twentieth century that her work has been recognized as timeless literature and extensive study applied to it. For these reasons, this check list is limited to criticism in this century. In addition, since the check list is an effort to record only criticism, general reviews of books about Emily Brontë and her work are not included, nor are general accounts such as those in encyclopedias. No fiction is included — in the form of novels, plays, poems, television and radio productions, motion pictures, readings, or juvenile treatments — whether adaptations of *Wuthering Heights* or versions of Emily Brontë's life. The books and articles in other languages (the third section of the list) were found in the course of research for the English part of the check list, and have been neither verified nor annotated. The items marked with an asterisk were unavailable for verification, but they may be accessible to a student working in another geographical area. Moreover, the check list is as complete as possible, but it is not exhaustive.

A listing of the Brontë manuscript material accessible to students in the United States and England has been compiled by Mildred G. Christian in her "Guide to Research Materials on the Major Victorians: The Brontës" in *Victorian Newsletter* 13 (Spring 1958), and her "A Census of Brontë Manuscripts in the United States" in *The Trollopian* 2 (Dec 1947) — 3 (Dec 1948) is invaluable for locating, in this country, Emily Brontë's manuscripts of poems. C. W. Hatfield's *The Complete Poems of Emily Jane Brontë* (1941) is the definitive edition of her poems, and William M. Sale's *Wuthering Heights: An Authoritative Text with Essays in Criticism* (1963) is probably the most accurate edition of the novel.

Primary source material, such as Charlotte Brontë's letters, may be found in Mrs Gaskell's *The Life of Charlotte Brontë* (1857) and Clement Shorter's *The Brontës: Life and Letters* (1908). It must be stressed that very little of Emily Brontë's own writing is extant; there are a few letters to Ellen Nussey, some diary papers, and several essays in French. Two of the diary papers and two letters to Ellen Nussey are in Clement Shorter's *The Brontës and Their Circle* (1917?); four diary papers are in Fannie E. Ratchford's *Gondal's Queen* (1955). Essays are translated by Lorine W. Nagel and introduced by Fannie E. Ratchford in *Five Essays in French by Emily Jane Brontë* (1948). A sixth essay is translated and discussed by Margaret Lane in *The Listener* 52 (Nov 11 1954).

For descriptive bibliography of the first editions of *Wuthering Heights* and *Poems by Currer, Ellis, and Acton Bell,* M. L. Parrish is very thorough in his *Victorian Lady Novelists* (1933).

Special help has been given me during my work on the check list by Dr Jackson Bryer, Department of English, the University of Maryland, and I appreciate the assistance of Mrs Frances E. Woodruff and her staff in the McKeldin Library, University of Maryland, and of Mr Howard Walker, The Library of Congress, Washington, D.C.

Bracketed pagination identifies those pages within the work which focus more specifically on Emily Brontë or her work. In Section A pagination is added for the few critical works wholly on Emily Brontë or on *Wuthering Heights.* For convenience, I have abbreviated — in my own comments in the check list — "Emily Brontë" as "EB" and *"Wuthering Heights"* as "WH." Three serial titles have also been abbreviated: [London] *Times Literary Supplement: TLS; Brontë Society Transactions: BST;* and *Nineteenth-Century Fiction: NCF.*

THE CHECK LIST

A Books and Parts of Books

Anonymous

A1 *The Brontës Then and Now* (Shipley [England]: Outhwaite Brothers 1947)
A symposium of eleven articles (ten of which pertain to EB) reprinted from *BST* and published as a *WH* and *Jane Eyre* centenary tribute. Annotated under the individual entries, the contents are as follows:
"The Three Sisters" by William Haley (B152)
"The Misses Brontë — Victorians" by Donald Hopewell (B174)
"The Haworth Tradition" by Ernest Rhys (B282)
"Influence of the Moorlands on Charlotte and Emily Brontë" by Butler Wood (B330)
"Ups and Downs of Celebrity" by W. L. Andrews (B31)
"Brontës through Foreign Eyes" [Originally "Through Foreign Eyes"] by Prince D. S. Mirsky (B237)
"Americans and the Brontës" by Helen H. Arnold (B32)
"Causes of Death in the Brontë Family" [Originally "Causes of Death of the Brontës"] by C. Mabel Edgerley (B111)
"Our Greatest Woman" by W. L. Andrews (B30)
"The Burial Place of the Brontës" by J. C. Hirst (B169)

A2 "Emily Brontë: 1818–1848" *Wuthering Heights* (Boston: Houghton Mifflin 1965) xv–xviii
A brief sketch of EB's life attributing the intensity of her emotions to a tubercular constitution.

A2a "*Wuthering Heights*, Emily Brontë" *Wuthering Heights* (New York: Airmont Books 1963) [1–4]
A short discussion of the novel and EB's life; the two Catherines give *WH* unity.

*   *   *

A3 Allen, Walter "The Early Victorians" *The English Novel* (New York: E. P. Dutton 1955) 153–252 [223–229]
WH is an "intensely individual apprehension of the nature of man and life," and Heathcliff is "a primordial figure of energy" rather than a monster. The double narrative is especially effective because it forces a role on the reader. EB anticipates Conrad.

A4 Altick, Richard D. *The Scholar Adventurers* (New York: Macmillan 1950) 316–317
In a chapter on the way that scholars have added to literary works, there is a brief discussion of the manuscript history of EB's poems and their Gondalan context.

A4a Anderson, Quentin "Introduction" *Wuthering Heights* (New York: Collier Books 1962) v–viii
"*Wuthering Heights* exhibits the realities of human life more clearly than any other English novel of the century." It has a moral order and a conventional order.

A5 Baker, Ernest A. "The Brontës — Emily and Anne" *The History of the English Novel* VIII (New York: Barnes and Noble 1936) 64–77
EB's personality is revealed through her poetry and *WH*. A full discussion of *WH* includes some possible sources for the novel such as Methodist magazines and the religious controversy in and around Haworth at the time the Brontës lived there, and the possibility that Branwell Brontë wrote part of it. The author says of the structure: "If it was clumsy to take the last events first, it was assuredly the clumsiness of genius." Reprinted: A104.

A6 Bald, Marjory A. "The Brontës" *Women Writers of the Nineteenth Century*
(New York: Macmillan 1923) 28–99 [77–99]
The part of this discussion concerning EB centers on the effects her poems and *WH* have on readers, with special attention to objectors to the novel and their reasons for objecting.

A6a Bell, MacKenzie "Emily Brontë" *Representative Novelists of the Nineteenth Century* I (London: MacVeagh 1927) 285–291
Most of this chapter is an excerpt from *WH*; a brief biographical sketch of EB and a short summary of *WH* is added.

A7 Benson, Arthur C. "Introduction" *Brontë Poems* (New York: G. P. Putnam's Sons 1915) iii–xx
EB's poetry is evaluated on p x–xvii. Her genius is "instantly apparent" and her poetry is clearly superior to that of the other Brontës. The interest the Brontë children had in writing poetry is attributed to Mr Brontë's writing poetry and to the books the young Brontës probably read.

A8 Benson, E. F. "The Brontës" in Derek Verschoyle, ed *The English Novelists* (New York: Harcourt, Brace 1936) *passim*
The traditional Brontë story with little about EB and *WH*.

A9 —— *Charlotte Brontë* (London: Longmans, Green 1932) 168–179
The evidence presented here that Branwell Brontë wrote the first two chapters of *WH* is based mainly on the style of writing; the style in these two chapters is compared with that at the end of the book. Both the beginning and the end of *WH* consist of Lockwood's narrative, and this fact is considered pertinent to Branwell's probable authorship. A section of this book is reprinted in A104.

A10 Bentley, Phyllis *The Brontës* (London: Home and Van Thal 1947) 83–102
The Brontës are investigated as to the material and equipment available to them (i. e., heredity, environment, inter-family influence, and education) enabling them to become novelists and poets. There is a perceptive treatment of EB's poetry, and a short treatment of *WH* from the point of view that "the story of Heathcliff . . . is a cuckoo's story."

A11 —— *The Brontë Sisters* (London: Longmans, Green 1950)
This short book touches on the qualities of the Brontë works which attract a wide range of readers, and is a brief factual account of the Brontë sisters' lives. It also contains a 4-page selected bibliography.

A12 —— *The English Regional Novel* (London: Allen and Unwin 1941)
On p 17 Dr Bentley notes that her selection of *Shirley* by Charlotte Brontë rather than *WH* by EB as the "first great English regional novel" may cause some surprise, but points out that *WH* is not regional, except in setting.

*A13 —— "Introduction" *The Heather Edition of the Works of the Brontë Sisters* (London: Wingate 1949)
"Highly interesting for its anticipations and psychological importance." [From an abstract in *The Year's Work in English Studies*.]

A14 —— "Yorkshire and the Novelist" in Richard Church, ed *Essays by Divers Hands, Being the Transactions of the Royal Society of Literature* n s XXXIII (London: Oxford University Press 1965) 145–157 [*WH passim*]
The diversity of the Yorkshire landscape and the characteristics of its inhabitants give impressive features to novels by Yorkshire authors which are set in Yorkshire.

A15 Blackburn, Ruth H. *The Brontë Sisters: Selected Source Materials for College Research Papers* (Boston: D. C. Heath 1964)
This is a bibliography of source materials for study of the Brontës. Section III, "Papers and Poems of Emily Jane Brontë and Anne Brontë," contains the diary papers and some of EB's

poems. Section IV, "Contemporary Reviews of the Brontë Novels," in addition to the reviews of *WH*, contains "Two Nineteenth Century Estimates of Emily Brontë," those of Algernon Charles Swinburne and Angus M. Mackay.

Blondel, Jacques *see* A131.

A15a Bowen, Elizabeth *English Novelists* (London: Collins 1946) 33–36
   WH, a book of "fire and ice," bearing no feminine stamp, is compared with *Jane Eyre* which "gains force by being woman from beginning to end."

A16 Bradby, Godfrey Fox "Emily Brontë" and "Brontë Legends" *The Brontës and Other Essays* (London: Oxford University Press 1932) 23–36, 37–50
   The first essay is a reprinting of Item B50. In the second essay, the veracity of some of the legends related by A. Mary F. Robinson in her biography of EB (1883) is questioned.

A17 Braithwaite, William S. *The Bewitched Parsonage* (New York: Coward-Mc-Cann 1950) *passim*
   This is a logical, objective, and intelligent account of the Brontë story, taking into account previous biographers' opinions.

A18 Bridges, Robert "The Poems of Emily Brontë" *Collected Essays* IX (London: Oxford University Press 1932) 259–268
   Referring to Clement Shorter's *Complete Works of Emily Brontë*, the author discusses the editions of EB's poetry to date. This is a fresh and perceptive evaluation of EB's poetry, but slightly distracting because it is written in a phonetic alphabet. See B98.

A19 Brown, Helen and Joan Mott "Introduction" *Gondal Poems by Emily Jane Brontë* (Oxford: Basil Blackwell 1938) 5–8
   EB's notebook which she herself entitled "Gondal Poems" was presented to the British Museum in 1933. This introduction to them discusses their history and significance. The value of the notebook itself lies in new poems and variants, new information on the Gondal story, new dates, and clues to EB's earlier poems. This edition of the poems was the first published from the manuscript in the British Museum.

A20 Burton, Richard *Masters of the English Novel: A Study of Principles and Personalities* (New York: Holt 1909)
   WH is very briefly dealt with (p 259) as "strangely unrelated to the general course of the nineteenth century."

A21 Cazamian, Louis "The Idealistic Reaction" *A History of English Literature, Modern Times* (London: J. M. Dent and Sons 1927) 345–368 [360–361]
   This chapter contains a brief and concise comment which credits *WH* with realizing "the ideal of independence in thought, and freedom in spiritual life, which the emancipation of Romanticism had set forth."

A22 Cecil, David "Emily Brontë and *Wuthering Heights*" *Early Victorian Novelists: Essays in Revaluation* (London: Constable 1934) 147–193
   This is one of the best analyses of *WH*: the famous "storm and calm" interpretation. The theme of the novel is the destruction and re-establishment of cosmic harmony. "The conflict is not between right and wrong, but between like and unlike." The individuality of *WH* comes from intensity, solidity, and spontaneity. The basis of this essay is that cosmic harmony contains elements of both storm (Heathcliff, and Catherine's separation from him) and calm (the Lintons and the love between the second Catherine and Hareton Earnshaw). Reprinted: A23, A104, A165, A194a.

A23 —— "Emily Brontë and *Wuthering Heights*" *Victorian Novelists: Essays in Revaluation* (Chicago: University of Chicago Press 1958) 136–182
   This is a reprinting of Item A22. The edition contains a new preface in which the author re-evaluates some of the Victorian novelists. He does not change his interpretation of *WH* and

EB except to say that she is, instead of "the most poetical of all English novelists," "*among* the most poetical . . ." (italics are his).

A24 Chadwick, Mrs Ellis H. *In the Footsteps of the Brontës* (London: Sir Isaac Pitman and Sons, Ltd 1914)

This is an encyclopedic study of the Brontës. Many details concerning their lives not mentioned or barely mentioned by other authors are included here. For example, the first five chapters give the ancestry and history of Rev Patrick Brontë, and Chapter XVII gives the history of M Heger. Of special interest to EB students are Chapters X and XXIV which deal with her career at Southowram and with *WH* respectively. Law Hill and the Southowram area are related to *WH*. The author gives careful evidence that EB stayed at Law Hill from 1836 to 1839, and discusses the poems she wrote while there. The authorship of *WH* is discussed at great length, and the conclusion is that EB is the only possible author. The idea that M Heger was the model for Heathcliff is lengthily supported by excerpts from Charlotte Brontë's novels and letters and EB's poems.

A25 Chase, Richard "The Brontës, or Myth Domesticated" in William Van O'Connor, ed *Forms of Modern Fiction* (Minneapolis: University of Minnesota Press 1948) 102–119

This is a reprinting of Item B71.

A26 Chesterton, Gilbert K. "Great Victorian Novelists" *The Victorian Age in Literature* (London: Williams and Norgate 1913) 90–155 [110–116]

Both Charlotte Brontë and EB had a false view of men, but Emily was "further narrowed by the broadness of her religious views."

A27 Christian, Mildred G. "The Brontës" in Lionel Stevenson, ed *Victorian Fiction: A Guide to Research* (Cambridge: Harvard University Press 1964) 214–244

This is an excellent and thorough discussion of the background and history of the Brontës, and one of the best surveys of Brontë manuscripts, editions, biography, and criticism.

A28 Church, Richard *The Growth of the English Novel* (London: Methuen 1951) 179–182

This is a very short treatment in which *WH* and EB are yet enigmas, and EB's poems are as "stark" as Blake's.

A29 Clarke, Isabel C. *Haworth Parsonage: Picture of the Brontë Family* (London: Hutchinson 1927) *passim*

The author states that this is an "attempt to present, in the form of biographical narrative, the tragic lives of the inmates of Haworth Parsonage." Some parts of the narrative are somewhat conjectural, but for the most part, it presents the traditional view of EB. Isabel Clarke was one of the first to suggest that EB was influenced toward mysticism by reading Ruysbroeck at Brussels.

A30 Clutton-Brock, A. "The Brontës" *Essays on Books* (London: Dutton 1920) 92–103

The author is primarily concerned with May Sinclair's *The Three Brontës* (see A177) with which he takes issue, with emphasis on Charlotte Brontë.

A31 Collard, Millicent Wuthering Heights — *The Revelation* (London: Regency Press 1960) 106 p

Subtitled "A Psychical Study of Emily Brontë," this is an imaginative, symbolical interpretation of *WH*. The characters all have counterparts in the Brontë family, and in its symbolic detail the novel is shown to be very closely related to the Bible.

A32 Collins, Norman "The Independent Brontës" *The Facts of Fiction* (London: Gollancz 1932) 174–188

In working with the Brontës, "Mrs. Gaskell is . . . a critical necessity" because their biography is so bound up with their books. *WH* is childish and the tale "leaps like a frog."

A33 Colum, Mary M. "Genius to Squander" in H. S. Canby, ed *Designed for Reading* (New York: Macmillan 1934) 103–111

EB and Charlotte Brontë are considered together. EB especially has "intensity which is one of the Celtic contributions to literature."

A33a Craik, W. A. *"Wuthering Heights" The Brontë Novels* (London: Methuen and Co 1968) 5–47

"Religious references (in contrast to principles) are frequent, because some theory of right and wrong and salvation is clearly being worked out," but EB is only using Christian references as a narrative method. What is required by EB of her characters in *WH* is "that they experience the full consequences of their actions." Dr Craik is primarily concerned with the characters in *WH* — their motivations, personalities, and effects on each other. Catherine's rejection of Heathcliff turns him from a passive person into a destructive force. Catherine and Heathcliff as characters are explicated in detail; they set themselves apart from the other characters and outside convention by contrast to brother and sister — Edgar and Isabella Linton, to husband and wife — Hindley and Frances Earnshaw; and they reject, separately, conventional Christian concepts. There is also a full discussion of the minor characters and EB's utilization of time in *WH*.

A34 Crandall, Norma *Emily Brontë: A Psychological Portrait* (Rindge, N H: R. R. Smith 1957) 160 p

Because EB had few friends and no proven lovers, "understanding the members of her family is not only the only certain method of portraying Emily, but is . . . essential in interpreting her writing." The author draws psychological conclusions such as: Patrick Brontë must have seemed "inhuman if not repellent" to EB, and, when Aunt Branwell died EB's feelings were probably "tinged with scorn." There is a 4-page bibliography at the end of the book.

A35 Crehan, T., ed Wuthering Heights: *With a Critical Commentary* (London: University of London Press 1962)

The force of *WH* lies "in the writing, in the presentation, and in the author's steady vision of her subject matter." In this well-detailed essay Crehan deals with the credibility of three elements in the novel: the misanthropy of Heathcliff, the love of Catherine and Heathcliff, and the characteristics of these two. EB uses the children, Catherine and Heathcliff, to make the adults more credible, and in her poetry we find anticipations of both of them. Crehan also discusses fully the chronology and law in *WH*.

A36 Cunliffe, J. W., et al "Charlotte and Emily Brontë," in J. W. Cunliffe et al, eds *The Columbia University Course in Literature* (New York: Columbia University Press 1928) 218–241

In this critical essay the stress is on Charlotte Brontë. As for *WH*, "it is a ghastly and gruesome creation. Not one bright ray redeems it. It deals with the most evil characters and the most evil phases of human experience."

A37 Cunliffe, J. W. "Charlotte and Emily Brontë" *Leaders of the Victorian Revolution* (New York: Appleton-Century 1934) 102–113

The author claims that, of the two sisters, Charlotte is the superior novelist; *WH* is barely mentioned.

A38 Daiches, David "Introduction" *Wuthering Heights* (Middlesex: Penguin 1965) 7–29

A thorough review and discussion of differing modern interpretations of *WH*, and a listing of some explicit points that anyone discussing *WH* should consider. The introduction is accompanied by notes and a selected bibliography.

A39 Davenport, Basil "Emily Brontë" *Wuthering Heights* (New York: Dodd, Mead 1942) 3–4

In this brief sketch of EB's life it is mentioned that Heathcliff may have been modeled on M Heger. *WH* may have been narrated by the heroine's nurse because Charlotte Brontë was ill when she returned from Brussels, and EB was her nurse.

A40 Dawson, William J. "The Brontës" *The Makers of English Fiction* (New York: Revell 1905) 124–144

The heredity and environment of EB and Charlotte Brontë are considered. The task of criticism is made difficult by (1) the influence of their personal lives on their work, and (2) the progress made by the art of fiction since they wrote. "The reading world" does not yet understand *WH*, but it is a classic.

A40a Day-Lewis, C[ecil] "Emily Brontë and Freedom" *Notable Images of Virtue* (Toronto: Ryerson Press 1954) 1–25

EB's work illuminates the idea of freedom, and is "a classic example of the way poetry moves from the particular to the universal." Reprinted: A165.

A41 Delafield, E. M., pseud [Edmée Elizabeth Monica De La Pasture] ed and intro *The Brontës: Their Lives Recorded by Their Contemporaries* (London: Leonard and Virginia Woolf at the Hogarth Press 1935) *passim*

Excerpts from contemporary nineteenth-century books, publications, collections of letters, and essays are placed in chronological order to reveal the lives of the Brontës. The section on EB is made up entirely of excerpts from Mrs Gaskell's *Life of Charlotte Brontë* (1857) and two of Clement Shorter's works: *The Brontës: Life and Letters* (A171) and *Charlotte Brontë and Her Circle* (1896). In the editor's preface, *WH* is criticized for lack of construction and a confusing double narrative.

A42 Dimnet, Ernest *The Brontë Sisters* trans L. M. Sill (London: Cape 1927)

This is a detailed, sympathetic study of the lives of the three sisters. Chapter VIII is an account and discussion of the stay in Brussels; Chapter XIV contains a perceptive investigation of the nature of *WH* — as a novel and as a work of art.

Dixon, Canon W. T. *see* A106.

*A43 Dobrée, Bonamy "Introduction" *Wuthering Heights* (New York: Collins Classics Edition 1953)

In this thorough examination of the flaws and excellences of Nelly Dean's role of narrator, her function is seen as not merely mechanical but also emotional because she is a part of the emotional texture of *WH*. Reprinted: A53.

A44 Dobrée, Valentine "Introduction" *Wuthering Heights* (New York and London: Knopf 1927) xiii–xxxv

WH is related to EB's poetry, and the grand scale of *WH* is attributed to her "preoccupation with metaphysical problems." EB "embraces her characters in a larger truth."

A45 Dooley, Lucile "Psychoanalysis of the Character and Genius of Emily Brontë" in H. M. Ruitenbeek, ed *The Literary Imagination* (Chicago: Quadrangle Books 1965) 43–79

This is a reprinting of Item B103.

A46 Drew, Elizabeth A. "Emily Brontë: *Wuthering Heights*" *The Novel: A Modern Guide to Fifteen English Masterpieces* (New York: Norton 1963) 173–190

This essay contains a brief review of modern criticism, which has rated EB's genius far above that of Charlotte Brontë. *WH*, however, remains mysterious; EB's own voice interprets nothing. Heathcliff loses the sympathy of the reader because of his inhuman cruelty. The fascination of *WH* is defined in Virginia Woolf's "unfinished sentence" evaluation (see A220).

A47 Drinkwater, John "The Brontës as Poets" *Prose Papers* (London: Mathews 1917) 118–130 [121–127]

The author questions the fairness of EB's genius as a poet having to carry with it the "dead weight" of Charlotte's, Anne's, and Branwell's poetry. He traces the development of EB as a poet, and he analyzes her poetry in order to separate the wheat from the chaff.

A48 Dry, Florence Swinton *The Sources of* Wuthering Heights (Cambridge: Heffer 1937) 48 p

This short book is an effort to delineate the sources of *WH*. The author points out the parallels between *WH* and Scott's *The Black Dwarf*; there are similarities of names, characters, revenge theme, and plot. There are also minor similarities to other Scott novels and to Shakespearean plays.

A48a Du Maurier, Daphne *The Infernal World of Branwell Brontë* (New York: Doubleday and Co 1961) *passim*

The author surmises that the germ of the idea for *WH* could have come from Branwell Brontë. She points out the Brontës' childhood habit of collaboration, but adds that the full credit for *WH* belongs to EB.

*A49 —— "Introduction" *Wuthering Heights* (New York: Coward-McCann 1955)

A50 Durrell, Lawrence "Lawrence Durrell" in E. W. Tedlock, ed *Dylan Thomas: The Legend and the Poet* (London: Heinemann 1960) 34–40 [38–39]

The author mentions in a short paragraph that EB's physical characteristics and her handwriting resemble those of Dylan Thomas. Reprinted: B108.

A51 Edgar, Pelham "The Brontës" *The Art of the Novel* (New York: Macmillan 1933) 136–145

This is a reprinting of Item B109.

A52 Elton, Oliver "Emily Brontë" *The English Muse* (London: Bell and Sons 1933) 365–366

This is a very brief analysis of EB's poetry.

A53 Everitt, Alastair "Preface" and ed Wuthering Heights: *An Anthology of Criticism* (London: Frank Cass 1967) vii–viii

Criticism of *WH* is marked by dissent about the essential meaning of the novel. Everitt notes in his preface that the various essays reprinted here reflect the complexity of *WH*, but they will not provide a solution to it. The collection includes:

"The Origin of *Wuthering Heights*" by A. Mary F. Robinson (1883)
"The Growth of *Wuthering Heights*" by Leicester Bradner (B51)
"*Wuthering Heights* and the Critics" by Melvin R. Watson (B320)
"Thoughts on *Wuthering Heights*" [Originally "*Wuthering Heights*"] by F. H. Langman (B195)
"Nelly Dean and the Power of *Wuthering Heights*" by John K. Mathison (B224)
"The Narrator in *Wuthering Heights*" [Originally "Introduction"] by Bonamy Dobrée (A43)
"Charlotte Brontë as a Critic of *Wuthering Heights*" by Philip Drew (B106)
"Infanticide and Sadism in *Wuthering Heights*" by Wade Thompson (B307)
"The Implacable, Belligerent People of *Wuthering Heights*" [Originally "Books in General"] by V. S. Pritchett (B264)
"On *Wuthering Heights*" by Dorothy Van Ghent (A192)
"The Style of *Wuthering Heights*" [From her book, *The Authorship of* Wuthering Heights] by Irene Cooper Willis (A208)
"The Structure of *Wuthering Heights*" by C. P. Sanger (A166)

A54 Ewbank, Inga-Stina "Emily Brontë: The Woman Writer as Poet" *Their Proper Sphere: A Study of the Brontë Sisters as Early-Victorian Female Novelists* (Cambridge: Harvard University Press 1966) 86–155

This very thorough treatment, which is of unusual depth, evaluates EB as "a Maker as well as a Seer." In *WH* her vision is a moral one. Miss Ewbank disagrees with David Cecil's contention (see A22) that *WH* exemplifies EB's philosophy of nature, made up of calm and storm; EB is primarily investigating the human condition, and the characters in the novel are moral beings showing the exploration of that condition. EB's sex does not matter because she is, above all, a poet. There is also a thorough review of nineteenth- and twentieth-century criticism, and a bibliography.

*55 Ewbank, Jane M. *The Life and Works of William Carus Wilson, 1791–1859*
   (Kendal [England]: T. Wilson) [pre 1959]

A56 Fadiman, Clifton "Afterword" *Wuthering Heights* (New York: Macmillan
   1963) 347–348
This is a brief and popular description of WH in which the author generalizes that the novel
is "a nightmare that makes perfect sense."

A57 Forster, E. M. "Prophecy" *Aspects of the Novel* (New York: Harcourt Brace
   1927) 181–212 [209–211]
After carefully constructing her WH on a time chart and genealogical table, EB introduced
"muddle, chaos, tempest" because she was a prophetess, and "what is implied is more important
to her than what is said." Reprinted: A131.

A58 Fulcher, Paul M. "The Brontë Sisters" *Foundations of English Style* (New
   York: Crofts 1927) 267–270
This is simply a reprinting of the part of Charlotte Brontë's "Biographical Notice" concerning
EB's death, with no comment.

A59 —— "Introduction" *Wuthering Heights* (New York: Macmillan 1929) v–xvii
EB's reputation has steadily grown for the last forty years. WH is compelling, but "the faults
of craftsmanship are as obvious as their corresponding merits." Nelly Dean is too literary and
the narrative method is complicated. Fulcher praises the way the characters are mirrored
in one another. There are perhaps in WH some minor incidents of EB's life; certainly the moors
are reflected in it. Although it is transformed, Hoffman's *The Entail* is the source of the plot.
When one returns to WH a second time "its full power appears."

A60 Garrod, H. W. "Editor's Introduction" *Wuthering Heights* (London: Hum-
   phrey Milford 1930) v–xiv
WH is a "novel of edification" for Mr Lockwood. He is the instrument of the moral of the
story: to teach the reader what love is. As for the scope of WH, "human nature cannot be interpreted . . . out of anything less than *all* nature." The story, however, is "ill-constructed, and in
its detail often complicated and obscure."

A60a Gérin, Winifred "The Authorship of *Wuthering Heights*" *Branwell Brontë*
   (London: Thomas Nelson and Sons 1961) 307–314
This modern, scholarly approach to the question of Branwell Brontë's possible authorship of
WH explores the evidence connecting him with the novel. The conclusion that he had no part
in creating WH is supported by examples of his prose and poetry, and by an analysis of his
personality.

A61 Gerould, Gordon H. "Interpreters: I. Hawthorne, Melville, and the Brontës"
   The Patterns of English and American Fiction; A History (Boston: Little, Brown
   1942) 341–366 [361–363]
WH is clumsy in structure and has technical defects. Nelly Dean keeps it rational, but the
"mad" characters are hard to believe. Nevertheless, EB accomplished what Melville "was to
attempt less successfully in *Pierre* only a few years later. No one has pictured better the dubious
battle of good and evil. . . ."

A62 Gettmann, Royal A. "Introduction" *Wuthering Heights* (New York: Random
   House 1950) v–xvi
This is a discussion of the position of WH as a Victorian novel. Nelly Dean is the prism for
the story; her purpose is "to control passions, bring out their meanings, and make them beautiful."
There are no set descriptions of nature in WH, for nature is "felt on every page . . . in phrases
and figures of speech." The theme of WH is found in Heathcliff.

A63 Gillie, Christopher "The Heroine Victim" *Character in English Literature*
   (New York: Barnes and Noble 1965) 124–134

Catherine Earnshaw is the focal point in this comparative criticism. Emma Woodhouse of Jane Austen's *Emma* and Catherine Earnshaw of *WH* are considered separately, then the two are compared as their authors' central characters. Heathcliff's credibility and five styles of "sexual emotion" in *WH* are also discussed.

*A64 Gleave, J. J. *Emily Brontë: An Appreciation* (1904)

*A65 Goodridge, Jonathan Francis *Emily Brontë:* Wuthering Heights (*Studies in English Literature* xx) (London: E. Arnold 1964)
This is an assessment of *WH* as fiction, not as other things. [From an abstract in *The Year's Work in English Studies.*] See A139a and A194a for partial reprintings.

A66 Gosse, Edmund "The Challenge of the Brontës" *Some Diversions of a Man of Letters* (London: William Heinemann 1919) 139–150
This is a reprinting of Item B140.

A67 —— "The Challenge of the Brontës" *Selected Essays* (London: William Heinemann 1928) 91–102
This is a reprinting of Item B140.

A68 Grabo, Carl H. "Technical Characteristics of *Wuthering Heights*" *The Technique of the Novel* (New York: Gordian Press 1928) 139–151
"Nature" in *WH* is more effective than "Nature" in Thomas Hardy's *The Return of the Native.* Lockwood intrudes and "is of no value whatsoever." Although the reader identifies with Nelly Dean, the devices which allow her narration of the story are thin. However, "the structural inadequacies are insignificant when weighed with its great merits."

A69 Green, John A. *Catalogue of the Gleave Brontë Collection* (Manchester: Moss Side 1907)
This is a valuable source for bibliography of Brontë works and nineteenth-century criticism.

A70 Grierson, Herbert J. C. and J. C. Smith "Early Victorians: Mrs. Browning and Others" *A Critical History of English Poetry* (New York: Oxford University Press 1946) 463–475 [467–468]
In this discussion of EB's poetry the authors conclude that she is "a more intense, if less variously accomplished, poet than Mrs. Browning."

A71 Groom, Bernard "The Brontës" *A Literary History of England* (London: Longmans, Green 1929) 345–348
There is a very brief reference to EB on p 346–347: "Emily's nature was more tragic than her sister's [Charlotte's], but it was also less rich," for Charlotte was the one who "usually kept her balance."

A72 Guerard, Albert J. "Preface" *Wuthering Heights* (New York: Washington Square Press 1960) v–xix
WH is a possible compensation for a life not lived, and is "a dark, splendid, imperfect novel." As an author, EB oscillates about the portrait of Heathcliff the reader receives; her treatment of Heathcliff, which is erratic and uncertain, is the novel's most disturbing structural weakness. Reprinted: A131, A194a.

A73 Haldane, Elizabeth *Mrs. Gaskell and Her Friends* (London: Hodder and Stoughton 1931) *passim*
On p 164 Charlotte Brontë's personality is compared with EB's.

Hanson, E. M. *see* A74.

A74 Hanson, Lawrence and E. M. Hanson *The Four Brontës: The Lives and Works of Charlotte, Branwell, Emily and Anne Brontë* (London: Oxford University Press 1949)

This detailed history, well-documented, of the lives of all four Brontës is a good starting point for any student of Brontë biography because it shows the effects the family members had on each other. Of particular interest to EB students are the chapters "Branwell and Emily," "*Wuthering Heights*," and "The Death of Emily." The major influence Branwell had on EB was her eventual reaction against his romanticization of life, which led to her own mystical belief that the final contentment of the soul is not found on earth. This belief is borne out in *WH* because the love of Catherine and Heathcliff is not an earthly love. In a thorough analysis of *WH*, the authors explore the role of Heathcliff, but determine that the two Catherines provide the vitality and human interest in *WH*, and indeed both give reality to Heathcliff. There is also a discussion of the prose and poetry of *WH*. From her letters concerning EB's illness and death, we can see that Charlotte Brontë understood neither *WH* nor Emily. There are careful notes and a 10-page bibliography.

A75 Hardy, Barbara   Wuthering Heights (*Emily Brontë*) (New York: Barnes and Noble 1963) 94 p
This book was written to be used as a teaching aid. *WH* gives the reader both physical adventure and "inner adventure." The inner adventure is effected by the reader's being required to sift evidence and make judgments. *WH* consists of two storytellers, two generations, and two worlds (supernatural and natural). Chapter XVII of *WH*, a transitional chapter, is analyzed in detail as an example of analysis and because the structure of *WH* can be seen in it.

A76 Harrison, G. Elsie *The Clue to the Brontës* (London: Methuen 1948) *passim*
The clue is "that the home of Thomas Tighe, who was Patrick Brontë's patron, was the Mecca . . . for Wesley's travelling preachers in Ireland." EB "could toss off the old childhood's tale [*WH*]" easily when Charlotte said the three sisters should all write books. It all came from Methodism lore. (See B157 and B13 for discussions of Methodist influence on the Brontës.)

A77 —— *Haworth Parsonage: A Study of Wesley and the Brontës* (London: Epworth Press 1937) *passim*
"Emily Brontë achieved her reputation on her Methodist background. . . ." An entry in John Wesley's journal is quoted mentioning the names "Lockwood," "Grimshaw," and "Sutcliffe," and the conclusion is that these names were the inspiration for the ones EB used in *WH*.

A78 —— *Methodist Good Companions* (London: Epworth Press 1935)
Chapter III, "Jabez Bunting," is about the man who has been suggested as the real-life model for Jabes Branderham in *WH*. Chapter V, "Reactions in Haworth Parsonage," alleges Bunting actually to be the model. The author says, "Methodism was Emily Brontë's nursery . . . her university also." She also finds parallels between Branderham's sermon and the character Joseph and the William Grimshaw legend.

A79 Harvey, W. J. *Character and the Novel* (Ithaca, N Y: Cornell University Press 1965) *passim*
WH is nearly a contemporary novel along with *Vanity Fair* and *Dombey and Son*, "yet they differ considerably in their mimetic relationship to life." *WH* is used as an example of narrative technique and novelistic structure.

A80 Hatfield, C. W. "Introduction" *The Complete Poems of Emily Jane Brontë* (New York: Columbia University Press 1941) 3–13
In this introduction to the definitive edition of EB's poems, Hatfield assumes the Gondal poems to be those in EB's notebook which she herself entitled "Gondal Poems," and he assumes that the poems in the other untitled notebook do not relate to Gondal. He says that the poems identify the mind of the genius who wrote *WH*. There is also a discussion of the ascription of poems not hers to EB. This work also contains sources from which the text of the poems has been derived, a list of books and magazines in which the manuscripts of EB have been printed in facsimile, and a list of words found in the manuscripts which have been altered to agree with ordinary spelling.

A81 —— "Preface" in Clement Shorter, ed *The Complete Poems of Emily Jane Brontë* (London: Hodder and Stoughton 1923; New York: Doran 1924) v–vi

". . . it is believed that we have now as accurate a transcript of the words written by Emily Brontë as it is possible to obtain." Hatfield's 1941 edition, however, is the definitive one.

A82 Henderson, Philip "Introduction" *Emily Brontë: Selected Poems* (London: Lawson and Dunn 1947) ix–xxviii

This is an explication of themes in EB's poems. Her poetry is compared to Byron's, briefly; although her poems contain the same satanism as Byron's, EB's poetry "explores those regions known to readers of St. John of the Cross as the Dark Night of the Soul."

A83 Hinkley, Laura L. *The Brontës: Charlotte and Emily* (New York: Hastings House 1945)

The author presents the facts, and her opinions based on these, in this careful recounting of the Brontë sisters' life story. EB is discussed on p 164–197, *WH* on p 318–349. Possibly a German story and a tale in *Blackwood's Magazine,* "The Bridegroom of Barna," influenced the creation of *WH.* Heathcliff could have been modeled on Joshua Taylor. EB's poems are seen as the Gondal story, except for twenty of them which are designated as personal. There is also a full bibliography.

A84 —— "Emily" *Ladies of Literature* (New York: Hastings House 1946) 175–211

This treatment of EB's life is similar to that in the author's *The Brontës: Charlotte and Emily* (A83). The treatment of *WH* differs in that it takes up the question of Branwell Brontë's influence on *WH:* the character of Lockwood was modeled on Branwell.

*A85 Hodge, Alan "Introduction" *Wuthering Heights* (London: Hamish Hamilton 1950)

A86 Hopkins, Annette B. *The Father of the Brontës* (Baltimore: Johns Hopkins University Press for Goucher College 1958) *passim*

This is a scholarly and sympathetic treatment of Mr Brontë. EB's "practical vein," shown in her skill at housekeeping, was probably derived from her father. On p 157–158 the author mentions the lesson in marksmanship Mr Brontë was supposed to have given EB.

A87 Howells, William Dean "The Two Catherines of Emily Brontë" *Heroines of Fiction* (New York: Harpers 1901) 228–239

This is a reprinting of Item B177.

Hughes, H. S. *see* A107.

A88 Jennings, Elizabeth "Introduction" Wuthering Heights *and Selected Poems* (London: Pan Books 1967) 5–13

WH "does almost all the forbidden things as far as nineteenth-century fiction is concerned," but EB brings them off by a force of vision. We learn more of EB's personality from her poetry than from *WH.*

A89 Johnson, James William "Nightmare and Reality in *Wuthering Heights*" *Wuthering Heights* (Boston: Houghton Mifflin 1965) vi–xiv

Physical nature and human nature are both stormy in *WH.* EB is concerned with the irrational, "that vast body of emotion which cannot be tested by logic or 'common sense.'" She uses dreams and ghosts to show the irrational. The elements of continuity in *WH* are landscape, weather, genealogy of the families, and a repetition of events. The characters, however, are the central nucleus.

A90 Karl, Frederick R. "The Brontës: The Outsider as Protagonist" *An Age of Fiction* (New York: Farrar, Straus, and Giroux 1964) 77–103 [77–90]

WH, a novel without hero or heroine, is held together by the doubling of structure and character, and the counterpointing of themes. There are many levels and contrasts in this novel. Also discussed is the place of *WH* in the history of the English novel, and it is compared with the novels of Austen, Conrad, Dickens, Lawrence, and Scott.

A91 Kavanagh, Colman *The Symbolism of* Wuthering Heights (London: John Long 1920) 30 p

This original treatment sees EB as a "Celtic genius . . . stimulated by keen domestic sorrow." In *WH*, Mr Earnshaw is father to Heathcliff and a hypocrite who leaves his family "a legacy of woe" in Heathcliff. Hindley, after Mr Earnshaw's death, proceeds on the principle of "an eye for an eye . . ." and Heathcliff reciprocates in the same manner. Hindley, for the unpardonable sin of despair, incurs the heaviest punishment of all, and Catherine Earnshaw commits the sin of pride, for which her daughter suffers humiliation. Edgar Linton, buried beside Catherine and Heathcliff, is their "good angel, unrecognized by them in mortal life, no longer between but for ever beside them."

A92 Kettle, Arnold "Emily Brontë *Wuthering Heights* (1847)" *An Introduction to the English Novel* (London: Hutchinson House 1951) 139–155

WH is "concrete and yet general, local and yet universal." EB works not in ideas but in symbols, and *WH* is compared with *Oliver Twist* in this respect. This is an analysis of *WH* that leads logically to the conclusion that the "feeling that binds Catherine and Heathcliff . . . is an expression of the necessity of man, if he is to choose life rather than death, to revolt against all that would destroy his inmost needs and aspirations . . . to become . . . more fully human." Reprinted: A104, A131, A194a.

A93 Kinsley, Edith E. *Pattern for Genius: A Story of Branwell Brontë and His Three Sisters, Charlotte Emily and Anne, Largely Told in Their Own Words* (New York: E. P. Dutton 1939) *passim*

The influence of Branwell Brontë on his sisters is narrated in the words and sentences of the Brontë novels; the characters in the novels are given the name Charlotte, Branwell, Emily, or Anne, but their words are the fictitious ones in the novels. The author says, "no apology is offered for transference in the following narrative of superb and well-known passages of prose from one setting to another, if such passages seem to have biographic verity." However, this biographical method is indefensible. *WH* and EB's poetry are used principally in Chapters V, VIII, XII, XVI, XXXII, XXXIII, and XXXIV.

A94 Klingopulos, G. D. "The Literary Scene" in Boris Ford, ed *From Dickens to Hardy; Pelican Guide to English Literature* VI (Baltimore: Penguin Books 1958) 59–116

EB is mentioned several times in this very general discussion of the Victorian literary world, e.g., "the novelists most free of the general dampness of the age are Emily Brontë and George Eliot." EB's poetry is compared with George Meredith's on p 95–96.

A94a Knight, Grant C. "The Most Terrible" *Superlatives* (New York: Alfred A. Knopf 1925) 20–39

Written for the potential reader of *WH*, this is a colorful and enthusiastic description of the novel and of Heathcliff in particular.

*A94b Lamont, William H. F. *An Analysis of Emily Brontë's* Wuthering Heights (New Brunswick 1938)

A95 Lane, Margaret *The Brontë Story: A Reconsideration of Mrs. Gaskell's Life of Charlotte Brontë* (London: Heinemann 1953) *passim*

This narrative story uses long quotes from Mrs Gaskell's *Life of Charlotte Brontë*. The author updates this valuable biography, using new material (e.g., the juvenilia) which was not available to Mrs Gaskell in 1857.

A96 —— "Introduction" in Philip Henderson, ed Wuthering Heights *with Selected Poems* (London: J. M. Dent and Sons 1907) v–x

Most of the poems are of no great worth; a few, however, are as beautiful as anything in our language. *WH* is a "long, intoxicating poem in itself," and its power lies in the ruthless love of Catherine and Heathcliff, made memorable by EB's own intense conviction of their existence.

*A97 Law, Alice *Emily Jane Brontë and the Authorship of* Wuthering Heights (Altham, Accrington: The Old Parsonage Press 1925)

A98 —— *Patrick Branwell Brontë* (London: A. M. Philpot, Ltd. 1923)
The case for Branwell Brontë's authorship of *WH* is carefully and calmly constructed in Chapter V, "*Wuthering Heights* — By Emily?" p 103–140, a collection of evidence for EB's not writing *WH*, and in Chapter VI, "*Wuthering Heights* — By Branwell?" p 141–184, a presentation of the evidence for Branwell's authorship.

A99 Lawrence, Margaret "Brontë Sisters Who Wrestled with Romance" *School of Femininity* (New York: Stokes 1936) 60–88
An apt subtitle would be "The Brontës and Their Men," because, according to this author, Charlotte Brontë and EB had a romantic attachment to almost all the men they knew.

*A100 Laycock, John W. *Methodist Heroes of the Great Haworth Round, 1734–1784* (Keighley [England]: Wadsworth & Co 1909)

A101 Leavis, F. R. "Note: 'The Brontës' " *The Great Tradition* (New York: George W. Stewart 1949) 27
A short note explains why he did not mention *WH* in his book: it seems to him "a kind of sport." Nevertheless, *WH* may have had some "influence of an essentially undetectable kind" on English literature.

A102 Leavis, Q. D. "Living at the Novelists' Expense" *Fiction and the Reading Public* (New York: Russell and Russell 1932) 235–273
On p 238 there is a very brief evaluation of *WH* as it looks to the book market: it belongs to the classroom.

A103 Lehman, Benjamin H. "Of Material, Subject, and Form: *Wuthering Heights*" in B. H. Lehman et al, eds *Image of the Work: Essays in Criticism* (Berkeley and Los Angeles: University of California Press 1955) 3–17
WH is not a Gothic novel; it is too universal. The material is nature and life; the subject is life renewing itself; and the form centers on Nelly Dean's character in the novel and her role as double-narrator.

A104 Lettis, Richard, and William E. Morris "Introduction" and eds *A* Wuthering Heights *Handbook* (New York: Odyssey Press 1961) v–viii
There are several possible approaches to *WH*: the characters in the novel offer a serious challenge to the reader, and other challenges are the action of the story, the point of view, the style, the symbolism, and the imagery. The essays (see individual entries for annotation) reprinted are as follows:
"*Jane Eyre* and *Wuthering Heights*" by Virginia Woolf (A220)
"The Structure of *Wuthering Heights*" by C. P. Sanger (A166)
"*Wuthering Heights*" [From his book *Charlotte Brontë*] by E. F. Benson (A9)
"Emily Brontë and *Wuthering Heights*" by David Cecil (A22)
"*Wuthering Heights*" [From his book *The History of the English Novel*] by Ernest A. Baker (A5)
"The Dramatic Novel: *Wuthering Heights*" [From his book *Representative English Novelists*] by Bruce McCullough (A110)
"Implacable, Belligerent People of Emily Brontë's Novel *Wuthering Heights*" [Originally "Books in General"] by V. S. Pritchett (B264)
"The Brontës, or, Myth Domesticated" [Originally "The Brontës: A Centennial Observance"] by Richard Chase (B71)
"Tempest in the Soul: The Theme and Structure of *Wuthering Heights*" by Melvin R. Watson (B319)
"Introduction to *Wuthering Heights*" [Originally "Introduction"] by Mark Schorer (A168)
"Emily Brontë: *Wuthering Heights* (1847)" [From his book *An Introduction to the English Novel*] by Arnold Kettle (A92)

"On *Wuthering Heights*" [From her book *The English Novel, Form and Function*] by Dorothy Van Ghent (A192)
"Nelly Dean and the Power of *Wuthering Heights*" by John K. Mathison (B224)
"The Narrators of *Wuthering Heights*" by Carl Woodring (B332)
"Emily Brontë's Mr. Lockwood" by George J. Worth (B333)
"*Wuthering Heights:* The Land East of Eden" by Ruth M. Adams (B22)
"The Villain in *Wuthering Heights*" by James Hafley (B148)
"The Incest Theme in *Wuthering Heights*" by Eric Solomon (B296)
"Lockwood's Dreams and the Exegesis of *Wuthering Heights*" by Edgar F. Shannon, Jr (B293)
"*Wuthering Heights:* Narrators, Audience, and Message" by Allan R. Brick (B55)
"The Image of the Book in *Wuthering Heights*" by Robert C. McKibben (B214)

A105 [Livingston, Luther S.] "Prefatory Note" *Poems by Charlotte, Emily, and Anne Brontë Now for the First Time Printed* (New York: Dodd, Mead 1902) v–vi
Most of these poems are EB's, and all of them are printed exactly as written with no effort made to edit them. Some are from the manuscripts written in a tiny script by the Brontës during their childhood.

A106 Lock, John, and Canon W. T. Dixon *A Man of Sorrow: The Life, Letters and Times of the Rev. Patrick Brontë 1777–1861* (London: Nelson 1965) 367–372
EB is supposed to be her father's favorite according to this well-written, but conjectural, account.

A107 Lovett, Robert M., and H. S. Hughes "Thackeray, Trollope, The Brontës" *The History of the Novel in England* (Boston: Houghton Mifflin 1932) 256–292
There is a short discussion of *WH* on p 283–285. It is yet a mysterious novel, "clumsily introduced" and told in a "style which is Emily Brontë's own." The story is "remote from human society." EB had a "tortured spirit" that is reflected in the love of Catherine and Heathcliff; their love is "both more and less than human."

*A108 Lucas, Peter D. *An Introduction to the Psychology of* Wuthering Heights (London: Guild of Pastoral Psychology 1943)

A109 Macaulay, Rose "Introduction" *Wuthering Heights* (New York: Modern Library 1926) v–x
A factor contributing to EB's personality and authorship of *WH* was the Brontë ancestry, having in it Celtic mysticism and imagination, and also the conflict engendered by mixed marriages of Catholics and Protestants in North Ireland. Nelly Dean's language in *WH* is sometimes too literary, but Joseph's is superb. Catherine and Heathcliff are "false men and women," but the author praises EB's "effortless power for creating atmosphere."

A110 McCullough, Bruce "The Dramatic Novel" *Representative English Novelists: Defoe to Conrad* (New York: Harper and Brothers 1946) 184–196 [190–191]
To its credit, *WH* did not fit the conventions for a novel of its time. This author investigates the major techniques used by EB in *WH* and the novel's major themes. Reprinted: A104.

A111 —— "Introduction" *Wuthering Heights* (New York: Harper and Brothers 1950) v–xix
This is an expanded and slightly altered version of Item A110, with a good survey of criticism of *WH*.

A112 McIlwraith, Jean N. "Introduction" *Wuthering Heights* (New York: Doubleday, Page and Company 1907) v–xi
"*WH* is Shakespearean in its impersonality. . . ." EB worked with a limited locale because "she could not paint a large canvas; her experience of life was too limited." The "taste for horrors" in *WH* is attributed to EB's reading the romances of Hoffman.

A113 Mais, S. P. B. *"Wuthering Heights" Why We Should Read* —— (London: Richards 1921) 25–31

Catherine's unforgivable sin in marrying Edgar Linton is "the attempt to sunder the body from the soul." EB was unerring in her psychology: her minor characters, Joseph and Nelly Dean, retain their individuality, and she could depict civilized over-refined people like Edgar and Isabella as well as the half-savages at Wuthering Heights.

A114 Malham-Dembleby, John *The Confessions of Charlotte Brontë* (Bradford [England]: Mrs Leah Malham-Dembleby 1954) *passim*
This author contends that Charlotte Brontë wrote the poems ascribed to EB and wrote *WH*, principally because he finds many similarities to Charlotte Brontë's novels in *WH*. Charlotte Brontë also wrote everything attributed to the other Brontë children.

*A115 —— *The Key to the Brontë Works* (London: Walter Scott 1911)
Among other allegations in this book is the one that Charlotte Brontë wrote *WH* as well as *Jane Eyre*. [Annotated from mention in *NCF*.]

A116 Margesson, Maud *The Brontës and Their Stars* (London: Rider 1928)
Viewed from strictly an astrological vantage point, EB is discussed on p 111–158. The planets and stars underscore EB's genius, introversion, and strong-willed individualism. The text is illustrated with astrological charts.

Martin, R. B. *see* A142.

A117 Masefield, Muriel "The Lives of the Brontë Sisters" and "Emily Brontë's Novel" *Women Novelists from Fanny Burney to George Eliot* (London: Ivor Nicholson and Watson, Ltd 1934) 95–128, 146–152
The first chapter stresses the importance of Mrs Gaskell's *Life of Charlotte Brontë* in any study of the Brontë sisters. The kitchen vignettes in *WH* and in Charlotte Brontë's novels are a reflection of the kitchen as a family center at Haworth Parsonage. The second chapter contains a review of *WH* criticism. Two features have made *WH* live: "the saturation of its characters . . . in the spirit of the moorland," and "the passion . . . which owes nothing to sensuality."

A118 Masson, Flora *The Brontës* (London: T. C. and E. C. Jack 1912) *passim*
The focus is on Charlotte Brontë.

A119 Matthews, Thomas S. *The Brontës: A Study* i (Dawlesh [England]: Channing Press 1934) *passim*
The story of the Brontë children is told, up to the end of the Brussels period, with particular attention to their endurance of financial hardships, their continual planning to better their lives, and their natural shyness which made it difficult for them to make friends. The appendix contains an essay, "The Brontë Parsonage Museum," by Marjorie Astin, p 115–118, which is a short description of the museum.

A120 Maugham, W. Somerset "Emily Brontë and *Wuthering Heights*" *Great Novelists and Their Novels* (Philadelphia: Winston 1948) 115–134
This is a reprinting of Item B225.

A121 —— "Emily Brontë and *Wuthering Heights*" *Ten Novels and Their Authors* (London: Heinemann 1954) 204–233
This is a slightly revised and enlarged version of Item B225.

A122 —— "Emily Brontë and *Wuthering Heights*" *Wuthering Heights* (Philadelphia: Winston 1949) vii–xxii
This is a reprinting of Item B225.

A123 Meynell, Alice "The Brontës" *Prose and Poetry* (London: J. Cape 1947) 97–108
This is a reprinting of Item A124.

A124 —— "Charlotte and Emily Brontë" *Hearts of Controversy* (New York: Scribner's 1917) 77–99 [94–99]

A few passages in *WH* are briefly discussed, and EB's poetic art of expression in the novel is evaluated. A possible source for the disinterment in *WH* is suggested. Reprinted: B232, B233.

A125 Miller, J[oseph] Hillis. "Emily Brontë" *The Disappearance of God: Five Nineteenth-Century Writers* (Cambridge: Harvard University Press 1963) 157–211

This chapter is one of the best modern interpretations of EB and her work. The author explains his point of view: "Post-medieval literature records . . . the gradual withdrawal of God from the world," and the five writers discussed represent the culmination of the process. For EB a "God of Vision" brought about a duality of feeling: wanting to be controlled by and yet control her "God." Her view of the world derived from her reading of Romantic literature and, to a greater extent, from her childhood religious training. EB's poems, her French essay "The Butterfly," and *WH* are investigated and compared. EB's philosophy is similar to William Blake's and John Wesley's. The other writers discussed are Arnold, Browning, DeQuincey, and Hopkins. Reprinted: A194a; partially reprinted: A139a.

A126 Millmore, Royston *Brief Life of the Brontës* (Bradford [England]: W. R. Millmore 1947) *passim*

The traditional Brontë story, briefly told.

A126a Moore, Geoffrey "Foreword" *Wuthering Heights* (New York: New American Library 1959) v–viii

It is because EB's "romantic imagination was ballasted by a shrewd grasp of human realities that the book has such a powerful effect."

A127 Moore, Virginia "Emily Brontë" *Distinguished Women Writers* (New York: E. P. Dutton 1934) 109–121

A dramatic and traditional biography of EB.

A128 —— *The Life and Eager Death of Emily Brontë* (London: Rich and Cowan 1936) 383 p

This biography of EB is somewhat histrionic and quite conjectural. One question raised is whether or not EB was Lesbian, and it is answered by the possibility that she was in love with a "Louis Parensell" (now generally agreed among most scholars to be "Love's Farewell" misread on a manuscript). In addition to this, EB, because of her unhappiness, was a "virtual suicide." The author suggests that EB had an early jealousy of Branwell Brontë, and assumes as fact that EB read certain books and magazines. The emphasis is on EB's introversion, loneliness, and unhappiness. However, in spite of inferences that are not supported by any known fact, the author quotes many primary sources such as Charlotte Brontë's and Ellen Nussey's letters. EB's poems are all seen as personal, even if they were written in the context of Gondal, and three new poems are printed here. One of the items in the book is a facsimile of the "Louis Parensell" manuscript. See also B159.

A129 Morgan, Charles "Emily Brontë" *Reflections in a Mirror* (London: Macmillan 1944) 130–155

This is a reprinting of Item B242.

A130 —— "Emily Brontë" in H. J. Massingham and Hugh Massingham, eds *The Great Victorians* (London: Nicholson and Watson 1932) 63–79

This is a reprinting of Item B242.

Morris, William E. *see* A104.

A131 Moser, Thomas C. "Introduction" and ed Wuthering Heights: *Text, Sources, Criticism* (New York: Harcourt, Brace 1962) v–vi

WH has modern appeal because the technique used is extremely intricate; moreover, it deals with subjects that are of interest in our century: the problem of evil and the power of the unconscious. In addition to the text of *WH*, this book contains thirty-five of EB's poems designated as those pertaining to *WH*, and a number of critical essays, as follows:

"Biographical Notice of Ellis and Acton Bell" by Charlotte Brontë (1850)
"Editor's Preface to the New Edition of *Wuthering Heights*" by Charlotte Brontë (1850)
"Prophecy in *Wuthering Heights*" by E. M. Forster (A57)
"Introduction to *Wuthering Heights*" by Mark Schorer (A168)
"Emily Brontë: *Wuthering Heights*" by Arnold Kettle (A92)
"On *Wuthering Heights*" by Dorothy Van Ghent (A192)
"The Minor Characters" and "Eros" [From his book *Emily Brontë: Expérience spirituelle et création poétique* trans Mary C. Moser] by Jacques Blondel (C5):

> The first essay deals with the method of narration in WH and with the characters. The narrative keeps the reader's attention on two levels which oppose each other: that of moral, everyday people and that of abnormal people whose actions are justified by passion. The characters can be placed in three categories: actors, victims, and witnesses. These, however, are far from rigid and a character may change from one to the other. The second shorter essay perceptively analyzes the passion in *WH*. Passion is self-affirmative, yet paradoxically it wishes to destroy its object.

"Preface to *Wuthering Heights*" by Albert J. Guerard (A72)
"What Is the Matter with Emily Jane? Conflicting Impulses in *Wuthering Heights*" by Thomas Moser (B244)

At the end of the book are suggestions for papers and a selected bibliography.

Mott, Joan *see* A19.

A132 Muir, Edwin "Time and Space" *The Structure of the Novel* (New York: Harcourt, Brace 1929) 62–87

An excellent classification of WH as a novel. As WH relates to the author's definition of Time and Space, it is a dramatic novel rather than a character novel, and it is a mode of seeing life in Time personally. There follows a good discussion contrasting WH to *Vanity Fair* and *Tom Jones*, and comparing it with *The Return of the Native, Moby Dick*, and other novels.

A133 Neill, S. Diana "Passions Spin the Plot" *A Short History of the English Novel* (New York: Macmillan 1952) 164–203 [171–177]

WH has something in common with a morality play because EB saw evil not as a positive force, but as energy misdirected. The symbolism in WH centers on the two houses: one is passion, the other reason.

A134 Newsholme, Sir Arthur *Fifty Years in Public Health* (London: Allen and Unwin 1935)

Background on the Brontës is given on p 17–22. The author, whose father was a churchwarden to the Rev Patrick Brontë in Haworth, relates stories of the Brontës he heard in his childhood. He also comments on the tuberculosis in the Brontë family.

A135 Newton, A. Edward "Brontë Country; My First Visit" and "Brontë Country; My Second Visit" *Derby Day and Other Adventures* (Boston: Little, Brown 1934) 297–306, 307–342

The first chapter is a first-person account, written for a popular audience, of the transfer of the Bonnell Brontë Collection to the Brontë Society, and the establishment of the Brontë Museum in Haworth Parsonage, with personal descriptions. The second chapter is an account, in a popular vein, of the author's education about the Brontës.

*A136 Nicholson, Norman "Introduction" *Wuthering Heights* (London: Paul Elek [Camden Classics] 1948)

A137 Nicoll, William Robertson "Introductory Essay" in Clement Shorter, ed *The Complete Works of Emily Brontë* i *Poetry* (London: Hodder and Stoughton 1910) xv–xlviii

Excerpts from letters and diaries by Charlotte Brontë and EB help make up the substance of a simple, condensed biography of EB. In addition, there are a review and discussion of criticism of WH, consideration of possible sources for WH, a discussion of Branwell's influence on his sisters, a contrast of the work of Charlotte, Emily, and Anne, and a discussion of EB's genius and her "personal faith or unfaith."

A138 —— and Thomas Seccombe "The Brontës" *A History of English Literature* (New York: Dodd, Mead 1907) 1165–1171 [1166–1167]
"WH . . . by reason of its sincerity, its freedom from affectation, triviality or verbiage of any kind, is, despite its imperfect or embryonic art, an almost unique book." There is also a reprinting of Henry James' short comment on the Brontës.

A139 O'Byrne, Cathal *The Gaelic Source of the Brontë Genius* (Edinburgh and London: Sands and Company 1933) *passim*
This is a reprinting, in book form, of Item B250.

A139a O'Neill, Judith "Introduction" and ed *Critics on Charlotte and Emily Brontë: Readings in Literary Criticism* (London: George Allen and Unwin 1968) 7–9
The introduction briefly traces the critical history of Charlotte Brontë's novels and EB's *WH* and poems. The essays and other material pertaining to EB are only partially reprinted (see individual entries for annotation in most cases).
"The Early Reviews" by Sydney Dobell, Lady Eastlake, and G. H. Lewes (1846, 1848, and 1850)
"*Wuthering Heights*" [Originally "Editor's Preface to the New Edition of *Wuthering Heights*"] by Charlotte Brontë (1850)
"*Wuthering Heights*" [From "*Jane Eyre* and *Wuthering Heights*"] by Virginia Woolf (A220)
"The Structure of *Wuthering Heights*" by C. P. Sanger (A166)
"The Style of *Wuthering Heights*" [From her book *The Authorship of* Wuthering Heights] by Irene Cooper Willis (A208)
"Emily Brontë's Romanticism" [From "*Wuthering Heights* after a Hundred Years"] by Derek Traversi (B311)
"The Metaphors in *Wuthering Heights*" [From "Fiction and the Matrix of Analogy"] by Mark Schorer (B290)
"The Window Image in *Wuthering Heights*" [From "On *Wuthering Heights*"] by Dorothy Van Ghent (A192)
"Nelly as Narrator" [From his book *Emily Brontë*: Wuthering Heights] by J. F. Goodridge (A65)
    Nelly's narrative has not only energy, but also a sense of reality because she uses concrete details. Goodridge explicates one passage from *WH* — Catherine's homesickness for Wuthering Heights when she is ill — to show how emphatic speech rhythms and plainness of language convince the reader of Nelly's veracity.
"The Rejection of Heathcliff?" [From "*Wuthering Heights*: The Rejection of Heathcliff?"] by Miriam Allott (B27)
"An Analysis of *Wuthering Heights*" [From "*Wuthering Heights*"] by Boris Ford (B126)
"Passion and Control in *Wuthering Heights*" by Vincent Buckley (B64)
"Infanticide and Sadism in *Wuthering Heights*" by Wade Thompson (B307)
"Themes of Isolation and Exile" [From his book *The Disappearance of God: Five Nineteenth-Century Writers*] by J. Hillis Miller (A125).
"Emily Brontë's Poetry" [From her book *The Genesis of* Wuthering Heights] by Mary Visick (A193)

A140 Paden, William D. *An Investigation of Gondal* (New York: Bookman Associates 1958) 85 p
This is another version of the Gondal story, with credit given to F. E. Ratchford's work on Gondal (A149) although Paden disagrees with her. A genealogical diagram accompanies this careful, well-documented treatment of the puzzle.

A141 Parrish, M. L. "The Brontë Sisters" *Victorian Lady Novelists. George Eliot, Mrs. Gaskell, The Brontë Sisters. First Editions in the Library at Dormy House, Pine Valley, New Jersey, Described with Notes* (London: Constable 1933) 79–96
This chapter contains a description of the first editions of *WH* and of *Poems by Currer, Ellis, and Acton Bell*. There are 1847 and 1850 editions of *WH* and two 1846 editions of *Poems*.

A142 Parrott, T. M., and R. B. Martin "Charlotte Brontë; Emily Jane Brontë" *A Companion to Victorian Literature* (New York: Scribner's 1955) 159–163
In this short account of both sisters' lives and works the authors say that *WH* and *Jane Eyre* "brought to the novel an introspection and an intense concentration on the inner life of emotion which before them had been the province of poetry alone."

A143 Phelps, William Lyon "The Mid-Victorians" *The Advance of the English Novel* (New York: Dodd, Mead 1916) 104–132
This is a reprinting of Item B262.

A144 Pritchett, V. S. "Introduction" *Wuthering Heights* (Boston: Houghton, Mifflin 1956) v–xiii
WH is the product of a mind which merged the blunt taciturnity and self-reliance of the moorland village people with their innate goodness. These are people who do not easily feel emotion, but when they do, they feel it for their lifetime. EB was unafraid to depict cruelty and torture: the elements of cruelty exist in the human soul, and the subject of *WH* is the self alone, or the soul. *WH* is Elizabethan in its intensity.

A145 Quennell, Peter "Foreword" *Novels by the Brontë Sisters* (London: Pilot Press 1947) vii–xvii
If Branwell Brontë did not write part of *WH*, he certainly had much influence over its author, and the Brontës from their childhood were experienced collaborators. In *WH* the human and superhuman are merged; details of setting and lighting are appropriate and unlabored.

A146 Ralli, Augustus J. "Emily Brontë: The Problem of Personality" *Critiques* (New York: Longmans, Green 1927) 1–16
This is a reprinting of Item B268.

A147 Ratchford, Fannie E. "Biography" *Wuthering Heights* (New York: Harper and Row 1965) v–viii.
A short biography of the Brontë family with attention given to the growth of *Jane Eyre* out of Angria and of *WH* out of Gondal.

A148 —— *The Brontës' Web of Childhood* (New York: Columbia University Press 1941)
This is the most authoritative study to date of the Brontës' childhood and their plays. EB: Chapters IX, XIII, XVII, XX, XXI, XXII, XXIII *et passim*. Appendix I is concerned with "Reconstructing Gondal," and Appendix III is "A List of Gondal Personal Names and Initials." A valuable aspect of this study of the juvenile manuscripts is that it points out their influence on the later writings. "Emily's one point of superiority was her full surrender to the creative spirit which Charlotte fought with all the strength of her tyrannical conscience." A bibliography of the Brontë manuscripts lists those of EB's poems, their location, and the location of the journal fragments and the birthday notes.

A149 —— *Gondal's Queen: A Novel in Verse by Emily Jane Brontë* (Austin: University of Texas Press and Thomas Nelson 1955) 207 p
This well-known work is the formulation of the Gondal story from EB's poems, and is based on the hypothesis that all the poems are related to Gondal. The author says, "the plot sequence of the poems and my own narrative prose links . . . are based on first-hand records, including all known literary remains of the four young Brontës." She presents a convincing case, although she does lean rather heavily on parallels in Gondal and Angria, in some instances, to support her premises. Gondal embodies ". . . on Emily's part a conscious and studied antithesis of philosophy and moral judgment advanced, no doubt, in protest against fallacies of the earlier creation [Angria]." The heroines of the Gondal poems are actually one heroine with several names.

A150 —— "The Gondal Story" in C. W. Hatfield, ed *The Complete Poems of Emily Jane Brontë* (New York: Columbia University Press 1941) 14–19

Hatfield's presentation of the poems "reveals that the majority, perhaps all of them, pertain to . . . Gondal." This conclusion would discourage subjective interpretation of EB's poems. Accompanied by a chronological outline, there is an arrangement of the poems as an epic of Gondal.

A151 —— "Introduction" *Wuthering Heights* (New York: Harper and Row 1962) xi–xiv
This brief history of WH publication also mentions major criticism of the novel, and traces the publications of EB's poems.

A152 —— "Introduction and Notes" *Five Essays Written in French by Emily Jane Brontë* trans Lorine W. Nagel (El Paso: University of Texas Press 1948) 5–8
The essays, written in Brussels while EB was studying with M Heger, "are in a very real sense autobiographical, sketching the fullest and clearest self-portrait we have of Emily." The introduction also gives the circumstances under which the essays were written and the dates of their composition.

A153 —— *Letters of Thomas J. Wise to John Henry Wrenn: A Further Inquiry into the Guilt of Certain Nineteenth-Century Forgers* (New York: Knopf 1944)
Thomas J. Wise, book collector and one of the editors of the Shakespeare Head Brontë, was discovered to be a forger. EB's manuscripts are not involved in the forgeries, but are concerned in Wise's collecting (p 23, 162–163, and 478).

A154 —— *Two Poems "Love's Rebuke" and "Remembrance" by Emily Brontë: With the Gondal Background of Her Poems and Novel* (Austin, Texas: Charles E. Martin, Jr — Von Boeckmann-Jones 1934)
The two poems are "Love's Rebuke" and "Remembrance." In the section entitled "Gondal: The Background of the Poems" (25 p, unpaginated), the author asserts that they are the key to the whole of EB's writings. The first poem is a lover's accusation and the second is a sweetheart's answer. The nucleus of EB's life and genius was the Gondal story, and EB's poems are closely related to WH.

A155 Raymond, Ernest "The Brontë Legend, Its Cause and Treatment" in Joseph Bard, ed *Essays by Divers Hands, Being the Transactions of the Royal Society of Literature of the United Kingdom* n s xxvi (London: Oxford University Press 1953) 127–141
"Almost every book on the Brontës is a fight . . ." and some of the people connected with the Brontës have been maligned by the biographers. This is a good defense of Mr Brontë, Aunt Branwell, and M and Mme Heger.

A156 —— *In the Steps of the Brontës* (London: Rich and Cowan 1948) *passim*
This is a modern story of the Brontës, especially related to scenery and locale. The "Introductory" provides a full discussion of what biographers have written about the Brontës in the past. The family legends she heard at Law Hill probably gave EB her ideas for WH. EB's poems are quoted to give a picture of her character, personality, and mysticism.

A157 Read, Herbert "Charlotte and Emily Brontë" *Collected Essays in Literary Criticism* (London: Faber 1938) 280–298
This is a reprinting of Item B277.

A158 —— "Charlotte and Emily Brontë" *Nature of Literature* (New York: Horizon Press 1956) 280–298
This is a reprinting of Item B277.

A159 —— "Charlotte and Emily Brontë" *Reason and Romanticism* (London: Faber and Gwyer 1926) 159–185
This is a reprinting of Item B277.

A160 —— "The Writer and His Region" *The Tenth Muse: Essays in Criticism* (London: Wyman and Sons 1957) 66–74 [69–71]
The universal and the particular are discussed as they are related to the moors and exemplified in *WH*.

A161 Reid, Stuart J. *Memoirs of Sir Wemyss Reid 1842–1885* (London: Cassell and Company 1905)
EB is mentioned several times, p 229–241, as Wemyss Reid's contribution to the interpretation of Brontë literature is reviewed.

A162 Romieu, Emilie, and Georges Romieu *Three Virgins of Haworth: Being an Account of the Brontë Sisters* trans Roberts Tapley (New York: E. P. Dutton 1930)
According to this emotional and sentimental treatment of the traditional Brontë story, the sisters were unable to love and be loved because they were deprived of their mother in very early childhood.

Romieu, Georges *see* A162.

A163 Rowse, A. L. "Afternoon at Haworth Parsonage" *The English Past: Evocations of Persons and Places* (London: Macmillan 1951) 143–164
An account of a personal visit to Haworth includes descriptions of the church and the weather, and retells the Brontë story.

A164 Saintsbury, George *The English Novel* (New York: E. P. Dutton 1913) 243
WH is mentioned as follows: "*Wuthering Heights* is one of those isolated books which, whatever their merit, are rather ornaments than essential parts in novel history." This is not true, however, of the works of Charlotte Brontë. Both the sisters made a contribution to the history of the novel in that they kept the novel and romance together.

A165 Sale, William M., Jr, ed *Wuthering Heights: An Authoritative Text with Essays in Criticism* (New York: W. W. Norton 1963)
This is probably the most accurate edition of *WH*; based on the 1847 first edition, it is a product of modern textual bibliography. The preface explains the edition, and the book also contains the following very helpful information: "Textual Commentary" 267–269; "Notes to the Text" 269–271; Appendix I, "A Note on Emily Brontë's Spelling and Capitalization" 271; Appendix II, "The Yorkshire Dialect" 272; Appendix III, "Emily Brontë's Copy of *Wuthering Heights*" 273–274; "Contemporary Reviews" 277–285; "Essays in Criticism" (see below) 286–378; and "Emily Brontë and *Wuthering Heights*: A Selected Bibliography" 379–380. The essays, annotated under the individual entries, are as follows:
"The Structure of *Wuthering Heights*" by C. P. Sanger (A166)
"Emily Brontë and *Wuthering Heights*" [In part] by David Cecil (A22)
"The Genesis of *Wuthering Heights*" [From her book *The Genesis of* Wuthering Heights] by Mary Visick (A193)
"Theme and Conventions in *Wuthering Heights*" by Clifford Collins (B76)
"Nelly Dean and the Power of *Wuthering Heights*" by John K. Mathison (B224)
"The Narrators of *Wuthering Heights*" by Carl Woodring (B332)
"Fiction and the Analogical Matrix" [Originally "Fiction and the Matrix of Analogy"] by Mark Schorer (B290)
"Emily Brontë and Freedom" [From his book *Notable Images of Virtue*] by C. Day-Lewis (A40a)

A166 S[anger], C[harles] P[ercy] *The Structure of* Wuthering Heights (London: Hogarth Press 1926) 23 p
This work is one of the milestones in the progress of *WH* criticism. *WH* characters have "a pedigree of . . . absolute symmetry," and it is printed here to prove the point. Not only the dates in the pedigree, but all dates in the story (nearly 100) are accurately interrelated. Mr Sanger, a lawyer, is quite qualified to comment on the English points of law bearing on the

plot, and he pronounces them flawless: The laws of entail and inheritance are strictly observed. A chronology is also printed with the essay. Reprinted: A53, A104, A165, A194a; partial reprinting: A139a.

A167 Schorer, Mark "Fiction and the Analogical Matrix" and "Technique as Discovery" in J. W. Aldridge, ed *Critiques and Essays on Modern Fiction, 1920–1951* (New York: Ronald Press 1952) 83–98, 67–82
The first essay is a reprinting of Item B290, originally entitled "Fiction and the Matrix of Analogy." The second essay is a reprinting of Item B291.

A168 —— "Introduction" *Wuthering Heights* (New York: Rinehart and Company 1950) v–xviii
In writing WH, EB is emerging from her Gondal, a world of "unmoral passion," to the real world which is a moral world. WH is a work of edification in which it seems the "cloddish" characters triumph at the end. The power of the book is that "yet the triumph is not all on the side of convention." The structure and the metaphors of the novel are also discussed. Reprinted: A104, A131.

Seccombe, Thomas *see* A138.

A169 Sharp, William "The Brontë Country" *Literary Geography* (London: Pall Mall Publications 1904) 106–124
This is a description of the Yorkshire area, interspersed with quotes from WH and Charlotte Brontë's novels.

A169a Shorter, Clement "A Bibliographical Note" *The Complete Works of Emily Brontë* I *Poetry* (London: Hodder and Stoughton 1910) v–vi
Before the appearance of the Shorter volume, only 39 of EB's poems had been published: 22 in *Poems by Currer, Ellis, and Acton Bell*, and another 17 in the poems printed by Charlotte Brontë after EB's death. 138 additional poems are included in this volume.

A170 —— *The Brontës and Their Circle* (New York: E. P. Dutton [1917?]
Material relating to EB is on p 132–163. This book contains letters of the Brontës which were not available to Mrs Gaskell when she wrote *The Life of Charlotte Brontë* — Charlotte Brontë's letters which refer to EB, two letters written by EB to Ellen Nussey, and some diary papers.

A171 —— *The Brontës: Life and Letters* (London: Hodder and Stoughton 1908) *passim*
Subtitled "Being an attempt to present a full and final record of the lives of the three sisters, Charlotte, Emily, and Anne Brontë from the biographies of Mrs. Gaskell and others, and from numerous hitherto unpublished manuscripts and letters," this work contains primary source material such as the diary papers of 1841 and 1845, two of EB's letters to Ellen Nussey, and Charlotte Brontë's letters to Ellen Nussey and W. S. Williams concerning EB's illness and subsequent death. The emphasis, however, is on Charlotte Brontë.

A172 —— "Introduction" and ed *The Complete Works of Emily Brontë* II *Prose* (London: Hodder and Stoughton 1911) v–xvii
Charlotte Brontë was the center of the Brontë literary picture when Mrs Gaskell published her biography, and Charlotte used her popularity to bring EB to the front also. The author discusses at length his editing of EB's poems in Vol I, and defends his policy of not correcting the poems. WH, as printed here, follows the first edition, and Joseph's dialect as amended by Charlotte Brontë is printed in footnotes. He suggests Patrick Brontë's early experiences in Ireland as a source for WH. Charlotte Brontë worked from models, but EB did not at all: her "genius was entirely introspective." The last part of the introduction discusses Mary F. Robinson's biography of EB.

A173 Simpson, Charles *Emily Brontë* (London: Country Life 1929) 205 p
This is one of the best biographies of EB, written "in the manner of a novelist," but he is not afraid to say "may have" instead of "must have." The biography is interwoven with local scenery and history — with Haworth, the moors, and the people concerned in EB's life. A

family history and star-crossed romance at Law Hill, where EB taught, are suggested as partial sources for *WH*. This book is original in that the author attempts to reconstruct, chronologically, EB's life, not as it has always been supposed to have been, but — on the basis of the evidence — as it may have been. Mr Simpson argues convincingly that EB may have taught at Law Hill in Southowram a much longer period of time than has been believed, and that this experience could have had a great effect on her maturity and her writing. EB's poetry is compared with that of Ruysbroeck, St John of the Cross, Wordsworth, and Coleridge. *WH* is discussed with reference to C. P. Sanger's *The Structure of* Wuthering Heights (see A166). The contents of EB's desk (the early reviews of *WH* and Newby's letter) are described.

A174 Sinclair, May "Introduction" *Wuthering Heights* (London: J. M. Dent and Sons 1921) vii–xiii

This account of EB and her work is told in an admiring manner. EB is compared with Charlotte Brontë in terms of personality, fame, and authorship. EB's poems were precursory to *WH* and it is in them that we see EB's "vision of life as she wishes it." Reprinted: A175.

A175 —— "Introduction" *Wuthering Heights* (London: J. M. Dent and Sons 1922) v–xi

This is a reprinting of Item A174.

A176 —— *The Three Brontës* (London: Hutchinson and Co 1912)

EB appears throughout the book, but she and her work are discussed in detail on p 165–240. The evidence supporting the author's conclusions about EB is authentic because it comes from Charlotte Brontë, Ellen Nussey, and the servants at the Parsonage. May Sinclair agrees with Maeterlinck's conception of EB as one whose "experience" took place in her heart if not in her life; she was a mystic with the power to weld love for earthly experience together with divine vision. EB's poems are discussed in relation to Gondal; the germs for *WH* are in them. There is a thorough treatment of *WH* that sees the roles of Nelly Dean and Lockwood as negligible, and points out Heathcliff's relative passivity in "letting" evil occur. *WH* belongs to no school; it is on the same mystic plane as the poems. (See also A30.)

*A177 —— *The Three Brontës* 2nd ed (London: Hutchinson and Co 1914)

This is a new edition of Item A176, with a new preface.

A178 Smith, J. C. "Emily Brontë — A Reconsideration" in O. Elton, ed *Essays and Studies by Members of the English Association* (Oxford: Clarendon 1914) 132–152

The publication of EB's *Complete Poems* in 1910 sheds more light on the Gondal chronicle, but it is as yet unclear. The newly-discovered poems contain "A Farewell to Gondal"; thus it seems that at this point EB is ready to write *WH*. *WH* is clumsy, but its greatness lies in its mysticism.

—— *see* A70.

A179 Southwart, Elizabeth *Brontë Moors and Villages from Thornton to Haworth* (New York: Dodd, Mead 1923) *passim*

The book is about the country and the natives of the area.

A180 Spark, Muriel "Introduction" *The Brontë Letters* (London: Nevill 1954) 11–26

The general background of the letters and manuscripts printed in the book is discussed here. The book contains EB's journal fragment, two birthday notes, and one of her letters to Ellen Nussey.

A181 —— "Introduction" *A Selection of Poems by Emily Jane Brontë* (London: Grey Walls Press 1952) 9–19

Swinburne noted three of the most important factors in EB's work: her instinctiveness, her primitive nature-worship, and her passion. These factors are developed in this essay as they relate to EB's poetry.

A182 —— and Derek Stanford *Emily Brontë, Her Life and Work* (London: Peter
  Owen 1953) 271 p
  Part I, a biography of EB by Muriel Spark, deliberately separates fact from legend and relates
  the life story based on facts, not on conjecture. Part II by Derek Stanford logically and precisely
  reviews the criticism of EB, her poems, and *WH*.

Stanford, Derek *see* A182.

A183 Stevenson, Lionel "Social Consciousness" *The English Novel* (Boston:
  Houghton, Mifflin 1960) 274–276
  This is a brief discussion of EB's poetry and of *WH*, with attention to the point of view pro-
  vided by the double narrative in *WH*.

A184 Stuart, Dorothy M. "Much Exposed to Authors" in N. Hardy Wallis, ed
  *Essays by Divers Hands: Being the Transactions of the Royal Society of Litera-
  ture,* n s xxx (Oxford: Oxford University Press 1960) 19–35 [32–33]
  The essay mentions the Duke of Wellington as he appeared in the Brontës' childhood plays.

A185 Sugden, K. A. R. *A Short History of the Brontës* (London: Oxford University
  Press 1929)
  This history was written because "people are beginning to write fanciful tales" about the
  Brontës. The author delineates five problems related to the Brontës, including the theory that
  EB did not write *WH*, and the "enigma" of EB and her work.

Symington, J. Alexander *see* A217 and A218.

A186 Symons, Arthur "Emily Brontë" *Dramatis Personae* (Indianapolis: Bobbs,
  Merrill 1923) 45–51
  This is a reprinting of Item B303.

A186a —— "Introduction" *Poems of Emily Brontë* (London: Heinemann 1906)
  v–x
  Symons sees "a sense, not of delight, but of the pain and ineradicable sting of personal
  identity" in EB's poems. She is a tragic figure whose "every poem is as if torn from her."

A187 Thomas, Edward "Emily Brontë" *A Literary Pilgrim in England* (London:
  J. Cape 1928) 269–274
  This description of EB's "country" focuses on her love for it, a feeling which is supported by
  Charlotte Brontë's statements. The author also points out the moorland in her poetry and *WH*.

A188 Tillotson, Kathleen *Novels of the Eighteen-Forties* (Oxford: Oxford University Press 1954) *passim*
  In the author's introductory chapter *WH* is used as an example of past-dating or past-setting
  employed in a novel to produce "aesthetic distance, underlining the distancing effect of Mr.
  Lockwood and Nelly Dean."

A189 Tinker, Chauncey Brewster "The Poetry of the Brontës" *Essays in Retro-
  spect: Collected Articles and Addresses* (New Haven: Yale University Press
  1948) 52–61
  This is a reprinting of Item B309.

A190 Traversi, Derek "The Brontë Sisters and *Wuthering Heights*" in Boris Ford,
  ed *From Dickens to Hardy. Pelican Guide to English Literature* vi (Baltimore:
  Penguin Books 1958) 256–273
  The author emphasizes the imaginative qualities of Charlotte Brontë and EB. The spirit of
  concentration found in EB's poetry is also in *WH*, and intensifies the "personal" or romantic
  theme. A second theme is "social" and is reflected in the contrast between Wuthering Heights

and Thrushcross Grange. The second part of this essay is similar to the author's "*Wuthering Heights* after a Hundred Years" (B311). Reprinted: A194a.

A191 Untermeyer, Louis *Makers of the Modern World: The Lives of Ninety-Two Writers, Artists, Scientists, etc. and Other Creators Who Formed the Pattern of Our Century* (New York: Simon and Schuster 1955)
In a chapter on Emily Dickinson (p 136–137) the author says Emily Dickinson has the "inner knowledge" of EB, and that a critic cannot tell how much of either author's works is based on experience and how much on imagination.

A192 Van Ghent, Dorothy "On *Wuthering Heights*" *The English Novel, Form and Function* (New York: Rinehart 1953) 153–170
The strangeness of *WH* lies in its ethical attitude, its level of experience, and its great simplicity (or lack of "the web of civilized habits.") Two "technical bulwarks" support the "uneasy tale": (1) the two narrators are both credible and commonplace, and (2) the story extends over two generations and ends with manners and morality. *WH* is related to EB's poetry, and the "window figure" and the "two-children figure" which are explicated in more detail in the author's essay of that title (see B314) are discussed. Reprinted: A53, A104, A131, A194a; partial reprinting: A139a.

A193 Visick, Mary *The Genesis of* Wuthering Heights (Hong Kong: Hong Kong University Press 1958, 1965) 88 p
This is a very thorough treatment of *WH* and the Gondal saga. EB's novel "arose . . . specifically out of the same material as her poetry," and both are discussed in great detail. This work is one that would be essential to any study of the relationship between *WH* and Gondal. There is an appendix of parallels, and a short annotated bibliography. Partial reprinting: A165, A139a.

A194 Vivante, Leone "Emily Jane Brontë 1818–1848" *English Poetry* (London: Faber and Faber 1950) 245–247
An objective, sensitive, and philosophical explication of EB's poetry.

A194a Vogler, Thomas A. "Introduction" and ed *Twentieth Century Interpretations of* Wuthering Heights (Englewood Cliffs, NJ: Prentice-Hall 1968) 1–13
According to the introduction, there are two contradictory ways of "seeing" in *WH*. One is Lockwood's and Nelly Dean's way, embodying common sense and empirical vision, and the other is Catherine's and Heathcliff's way, vision beyond the limits of reality. "What both extremes overlook is the possibility that the novel is about the problem of contrasted vision itself, perhaps even about the impossibility of adopting decisively one or the other mode of vision." Vogler includes a chronology and a selected bibliography. The critical essays (annotated in the individual entries in most cases) are as follows:
"The Structure of *Wuthering Heights*" by Charles Percy Sanger (A166)
"Emily Brontë: *Wuthering Heights*" by Arnold Kettle (A92)
"Fiction and the Matrix of Analogy" by Mark Schorer (B290)
"The Brontë Sisters and *Wuthering Heights*" by Derek Traversi (A190)
"Preface to *Wuthering Heights*" by Albert J. Guerard (A72)
"The Circumambient Universe" [From his book *Emily Brontë*: Wuthering Heights] by J. Frank Goodridge (A65)
> In a discussion of Nature in *WH*, the two rival houses, and worlds of heaven and hell, Goodridge says, "the exposed wilderness of unreclaimed nature is . . . the rock beneath the cultivated soil of human life. . . ." The two houses show two possible ways of living. A number of private heavens and hells are contrasted, and in this connection, the author investigates Lockwood, Hindley, Heathcliff, Catherine, Cathy, Joseph, Isabella, and Edgar.
"Story and History in *Wuthering Heights*" by Thomas A. Vogler
> A penetrating look at Lockwood and through Lockwood clearly demonstrates that any assumption of a resolution in *WH* is a repudiation of the essential theme of the novel, which consists of contraries, and the process of change is the reality behind the events in the novel.
"*Jane Eyre* and *Wuthering Heights*" by Virginia Woolf (A220)

"Emily Brontë and *Wuthering Heights*" by David Cecil (A22)
"On *Wuthering Heights*" by Dorothy Von Ghent (A192)
"Lockwood's Dreams and the Exegesis of *Wuthering Heights*" by Edgar F. Shannon, Jr (B293)
"Implacable, Belligerent People of Emily Brontë's Novel, *Wuthering Heights*" by V. S. Pritchett (B264)
"Introduction to *Wuthering Heights*" by David Daiches (A38)
"The Incest Theme in *Wuthering Heights*" by Eric Solomon (B296)
"Emily Brontë and the Metaphysics of Childhood and Love" by Irving H. Buchen (B61)
"Emily Brontë" by J. Hillis Miller (A125)

A195 Wagenknecht, Edward C. "Fire over Yorkshire" *Cavalcade of the English Novel* (New York: Holt 1943) 304–318; second edition (New York: Holt 1954)
The contributions of Charlotte Brontë and EB to English fiction are evaluated; there is also a thorough review of Brontë criticism to date and a bibliography. (The later edition, 1954, contains a supplementary bibliography of materials on the Brontës.)

A196 Walker, Hugh "The Brontës" *The Literature of the Victorian Era* (London: Cambridge University Press 1910) 723–724
EB was inferior to Charlotte Brontë as an artist, and even had she lived longer, "she might have proved an intractable pupil and have marred other novels as she marred *Wuthering Heights* by the very excess of the qualities which made her great."

A197 Walker, Mrs J. R. "The Brontës" *Stories of the Victorian Writers* (London: Cambridge University Press 1922) 77–85
The author tells the traditional Brontë story and briefly discusses EB's poetry. She relates a legend about Hugh Brontë's adoption of an orphaned Welsh boy, similar to the story of Heathcliff in *WH*.

A198 Walters, J. Cuming *The Spell of Yorkshire* (London: Methuen and Co 1931)
On p 98–118 the author gives a depressing view of all the Brontës in the context of a gloomy geographical area.

A199 Ward, Mrs Humphry "Introduction" *Wuthering Heights* (New York and London: Harper and Brothers 1903) xi–xl
Mrs Ward opposes the opinions of George Saintsbury and Leslie Stephen regarding **WH**, and says that the novel has not yet taken the place that rightly belongs to it. She wishes, however, for a more "flowing unity" in *WH*. It belongs to the "later Romantic movement." EB's genius is attributed to her Celtic blood, and she was influenced by German literature. EB's poetry is briefly discussed. Reprinted: B318.

A200 Watson, Melvin R. "Form and Substance in the Brontë Novels" in Robert C. Rathburn and Martin Steinmann, Jr, eds *From Jane Austen to Joseph Conrad* (Minneapolis: University of Minnesota Press 1958) 106–117
WH and *Jane Eyre* survive as classics because their form and their substance are welded together; in the other Brontë novels form and substance are at war. EB excluded everything not pertinent to her theme in *WH*, and her timing is remarkable. *WH* is the greatest of the Brontë novels, he says, but for the most part he discusses Charlotte Brontë's work.

A201 —— "Tempest in the Soul: The Theme and Structure of *Wuthering Heights*" in Austin Wright, ed *Victorian Literature: Modern Essays in Criticism* (New York: Oxford University Press 1961) 86–97
This is a reprinting of Item B319.

A202 Weygandt, Cornelius "The Spectacle of the Brontës" *A Century of the English Novel* (New York: Century 1925) 102–121
Jane Eyre and *WH* are books to be reread because of their intensity of emotion. *WH*'s "survival as a classic is assured despite its burden of absurdities." The lyricism in the novel contributes much to the enjoyment of rereadings of *WH*, and the reader tends to forget the brutalities of the story.

A203 White, W. Bertram *The Miracle of Haworth: A Brontë Study* (London: University of London Press 1937)

This is a general study of the Brontë family, with a 5-page bibliography. Chapter X, "Emily Is Changed," asserts that EB refused to return to Brussels with Charlotte Brontë because of the death of William Weightman. "This was undoubtedly the loss which completely altered Emily's whole outlook on life. . . ." Mr Weightman is subsequently given credit for the passion found in some of EB's poems and for "a love that can triumph over death" in *WH*. EB's reading at Brussels probably included Ruysbroeck, St Therese, and St John of the Cross from whom she learned "the language of mysticism." Chapter XVII, *"Wuthering Heights,"* praises EB's acute observation of and use of the natural setting of the moors in her novel, but attributes the novel's greatness to the love of Catherine and Heathcliff, which was like that of Dante and Beatrice. The author also discusses Branwell Brontë's influence on *WH* and compares EB to many other female writers and poets.

A204 Whitehead, Phyllis *The Brontës Came Here* (Halifax: Fawcett, Greenwood and Co 1965)

In this guide to most of the north-country places associated with the Brontës, an effort is made to connect sites and buildings with those in the Brontë novels, e.g., Wuthering Heights and Thrushcross Grange.

A205 Whitmore, Clara H. *Woman's Work in English Fiction* (New York: Putnam 1910)

On p 249–257, *WH* and EB's poetry are discussed. Catherine is compared with Undine. During the three years of her marriage to Edgar Linton, Catherine's "better nature triumphs." Heathcliff is "capable of a love stronger than his hate."

A206 Willcocks, M. P. "Charlotte and Emily Brontë" *Between the Old World and the New* (London: Allen and Unwin 1925) 157–168

The author evaluates both EB and Charlotte Brontë; she points out the value of EB's escape into her inner world, the strength and mysticism of that world, and her absolute independence from the Victorian world and its creeds.

A206a Williams, A. M. "Emily Brontë" *Our Early Female Novelists and Other Essays* (Glasgow: J. MacLehose and Sons 1904) 65–85

The major influences on EB's work were the moors, her father, Miss Branwell, and Tabby. The promise of *WH* is in the delineation of character rather than the story. EB's poetry lacks form and some of the poems have a "certain gloom," but attractive characteristics of them are a feeling for nature, pensiveness, and grandeur of thought.

A207 Williams, Harold "The Brontë Sisters" *Two Centuries of the English Novel* (London: Smith, Elder 1911) 215–233 [218–228]

EB "was pagan in temperament and creed" and felt "neither hope nor optimism. . . ." The characters in *WH* "are abnormal in an abnormal setting. . . ."

A208 Willis, Irene Cooper *The Authorship of* Wuthering Heights (London: Hogarth Press 1936) 94 p

The purpose of this book is to present the evidence against Branwell Brontë's authorship of *WH*. Part I discusses *WH*, pointing out the usefulness and value of the character Lockwood, and describing the effect achieved by the double narrative of the story. Part II, "Branwell Brontë's Writings," quotes his work and shows why he could not have written *WH*. Sections of this book are reprinted in A53, A139a.

A209 —— *The Brontës* (London: Duckworth 1933)

This is a short history of the Brontës. EB is discussed in Chapters V, VI, and VII. She was "difficult to live with," and wanted freedom from people; "freedom was the breath of her soul," but she was lonely. *WH* is evaluated in Chapter VII as primitive and realistic. The advantages and disadvantages of narration through Nelly Dean and Lockwood are discussed at length. Heathcliff was not monstrous in EB's eyes, and "Mrs. Dean's occasional inclination to see him as such has to be discounted"; after all, Lockwood at times enjoyed his company.

*A210 Willy, Margaret *A Critical Commentary on Emily Brontë's* Wuthering Heights (London: Macmillan 1966) 79 p

A211 —— "The Poetry of Emily Dickinson" *Essays and Studies 1957* n s x (London: John Murray 1957) 91–104
This is a comparison of Emily Dickinson's poetry with that of EB, with emphasis on EB's influence on Emily Dickinson.

A212 Wilson, Romer, pseud [Florence Roma Muir (Wilson) O'Brien] *All Alone: The Life and Private History of Emily Jane Brontë* (London: Chatto and Windus 1928) 298 p
This very personal interpretation of EB evaluates her life in an effort to explain her genius; therefore, most of the book is of necessity conjectural. The influence of the moors and EB's family environment are both seen as unhappy factors in her life, but they also created an individual capable of writing *WH*. Reflecting the tone of the rest of the book, Appendix IV is a list of EB's "poems of guilt."

A213 Wise, Thomas J. *The Ashley Library: A Catalogue of Printed Books, Manuscripts and Autograph Letters* (Edinburgh: Dunedin Press 1922)
On p 82 there is a descriptive bibliography of EB's holograph poems and editions of *WH* and *Poems* edited by Clement Shorter.

A214 —— *A Bibliography of the Writings in Prose and Verse of the Members of the Brontë Family* (London: Clay and Sons 1917)
Part II, "Emily and Anne Brontë," is a descriptive bibliography. The fifteen corrections in the edition of *WH* owned by Clement Shorter, which are supposed to be in EB's own handwriting, are listed.

A215 —— *A Brontë Library: A Catalogue of Printed Books, Manuscripts and Autograph Letters by the Members of the Brontë Family* (London: Dunedin Press 1929)
Part II, "The Writings of Emily Jane Brontë," is a descriptive bibliography.

*A216 —— *Letters Recounting the Deaths of Emily, Anne and Branwell Brontë by Charlotte Brontë* [A pamphlet] 1913

A217 —— and J. Alexander Symington "Preface" and eds *The Brontës: Their Lives, Friendships and Correspondence* 4 vols [Shakespeare Head Brontë] (Oxford: Basil Blackwell 1932) i vii–ix
The brief mention of EB is as follows "Emily Brontë is now recognized as affording one of the most interesting studies of womanhood, and her poetry ranks high in English literature."

A218 —— "Preface" *The Poems of Emily Jane Brontë and Anne Brontë* (Oxford: Shakespeare Head Press 1934) ix–xii
A survey of the history of the publication of EB's poems, with a bibliography of EB's and Anne Brontë's works.

A219 Woodberry, George E. "The Brontë Novels" *Studies of a Litterateur* (New York: Harcourt, Brace 1921) 253–260
A very perceptive evaluation of EB and Charlotte. The Brontës' "reputation remains side by side with Jane Austen's"; Mrs Humphry Ward's "Introduction" (see A199) is cited as the best criticism of the Brontës.

A220 Woolf, Virginia "*Jane Eyre* and *Wuthering Heights*" *The Common Reader: First Series* (London: Hogarth Press 1925) 196–204 [201–204]

EB poses a question with her novel which she does not answer. Virginia Woolf paraphrases *WH*: ". . . not merely 'I love' or 'I hate,' but 'we, the whole human race' and 'you, the eternal powers. . . .' the sentence remains unfinished." EB could, however, "free life from its dependence upon facts." Reprinted A104, A194a; partial reprinting: A139a.

A221 Wright, J. C. *The Story of the Brontës* (London: Leonard Parsons 1925)
There are two chapters pertinent to EB: the first, "*Wuthering Heights*," reviews the past and present criticism of the novel, particularly that of J. Malham-Dembleby who claims that Charlotte Brontë wrote *WH*; in the second, "Emily Brontë and Her Poetry," the author compares her poems with those of Wordsworth and Meredith.

A222 Wyatt, Edith "Brontë Poems" *Great Companions* (New York: Appleton-Century 1917) 191–197 [195–197]
". . . the Brontë's lives are read into their work and their work into their lives until neither has any distinct or integral value." Fragments of the Brontë poems are quoted to support the theory that artistic creation need not be based upon experience.

B   Articles

Anonymous

B1 "Another Brontë Discovery" *Literary Digest* 48 (Apr 4 1914) 759
This article announces the discovery in Ireland of two Brontë portraits — one of EB and the other of the three Brontë sisters — painted by Branwell Brontë.

B2 "Brontë Discoveries" *Bookman* (New York) 33 (May 1911) 228
A report of J. Malham-Dembleby's discoveries of correlations between Charlotte Brontë's [sic] *Wuthering Heights* and *Jane Eyre* accompanied by a Tourist's Guide to the Brontë country.

B3 "Brontës Are Earning a New Popularity" *Life* 15 (Nov 29 1943) 95–103
The traditional story of the Brontës is told alongside photographs of the supposed farmhouse model for Wuthering Heights, photographs of Haworth Parsonage, and engravings depicting the story of *WH*.

B4 "Drawings by Emily Brontë of Geometrical Problems, Signed and Dated 'September the 9th 1837'" *BST* 14 (1962) Plate 11
The drawings are reproduced without comment.

*B5 "Emily Brontë" *TLS* [pre Jan 30 1909]
EB is the enigma in the Brontë family although we can know her to some extent through her poems. The power of *WH* lies in its threadbare truth which is unadorned by any "romantic beauty" of landscape. Reprinted: B6.

B6 "Emily Brontë" *Living Age* 260 (Jan 30 1909) 302–308
This is a reprinting of Item B5.

B7 "Emily Brontë" *TLS* (Dec 18 1948) 713
This centenary article about EB, her character, and *WH* concludes that "the unsolved mystery [of EB and *WH*] is the eternal one of genius."

B8 "Emily Brontë: A Diary Paper" *BST* 12 (1951) 15
The diary fragment which was dated June 26 1837 is deciphered here; the frontispiece of this volume is a facsimile of the original.

B9 "A First Edition of *Wuthering Heights*" *BST* 14 (1964) 50
A description of the Newby 1847 edition of *WH* with penciled corrections in the first volume, which was sold at auction in July 1964. The corrections are believed to be Charlotte Brontë's.

B10 "The Genius of the Moors" *Academy and Literature* 65 (Oct 3 1903) 333–334
Regarding the controversy about Branwell Brontë's authorship of *WH*, this author asserts
that *WH* was written by a woman, and gives internal evidence: Mr Lockwood's point of view
is never that of a man. Moreover, EB's poetry reveals her to be the only possible author of *WH*.

B11 "Landscape in the Brontë Novels" *The Academy* 71 (Sept 8 1906) 226–228
EB's descriptions of scenery in *WH* are brief, but "extraordinarily effective" and essential
to the plot.

B11a "The 150th Anniversary of the Birth of Emily Jane Brontë" *BST* 15 (1968)
201–205
A description of the anniversary, which was marked by ceremonies in Haworth and at Westminster Abbey, with the commemorative addresses given by Naomi Lewis and Donald Hopewell.

B12 "Patrick Branwell Brontë and *Wuthering Heights*" *BST* 7 (1927) 97–102
The article ascribing the authorship of *WH* to Branwell Brontë which appeared in *The Halifax Guardian* dated June 15 1867 is reprinted here because it is "too little known in its entirety
and . . . difficult to obtain."

B13 "Pot-Shooting" *TLS* (Apr 30 1949) 281
An article in which the *TLS* editor puts a stop to a controversy (see B164) about EB's
poem "The Visionary," because of the excessive amount of conjecture. The writer mentions the
Methodist influence on the Brontës emphasized by G. Elsie Harrison (see A76). See B117
for a reply.

B14 "The 'Splendid Isolation' of Emily Brontë" *Current Literature* 40 (May 1906)
512
This is a brief review of nineteenth-century criticism of *WH* with special attention to Clement
Shorter's evaluation of the novel.

B15 "Three Essays by Emily Brontë" *BST* 11 (1950) 337–341
"The Cat," "The Butterfly," and "Letter from One Brother to Another," translated from the
French by Lorine W. Nagel. These essays are in addition to the two French essays in the Bon-
nell Collection (see B81); all five are included in F. E. Ratchford's booklet (A152). See also
B193, B194.

B16 "Two Brussels Schoolfellows of Charlotte Brontë" *BST* 5 (Apr 1913) 25–29
This article recalls two schoolmates of Emily and Charlotte Brontë, and reprints Miss Wheel-
wright's impression of EB, which was not flattering.

B17 "An Unrecovered Poetess" *TLS* (June 10 1915) 189
EB's courageous poetry is made timely by World War I. As a poet she is compared with
William Blake. Unfortunately, she continually attempted to write an "English" poem, and did
not know where her true talent lay. She made the mistake of striving for a "conventional
finish." Reprinted: B18.

B18 "An Unrecovered Poetess" *Living Age* 286 (July 24 1915) 216–222
This is a reprinting of Item B17.

B19 "Where the Brontës Borrowed Books: The Keighley Mechanics Institute"
BST 11 (1950) 344–358
A discussion of the possible sources of the pseudonyms "Currer" and "Ellis," and a catalogue
of the books available at the Institute in 1841.

*   *   *

B19a A., W. L. "An Emily Brontë Excursion, 1968" *BST* 15 (1968) 262
The Society's annual excursion was to Shibden Hall, Law Hill House, and the site of High
Sunderland Hall. Donald Hopewell spoke about the scenic and architectural background of

WH, designating High Sunderland Hall as the model for Wuthering Heights and Shibden Hall for Thrushcross Grange.

B20 Abercrombie, Lascelles "The Brontës Today" *BST* 6 (1924) 179–200 [196–200]
   A biographical and critical discussion of the Brontës. ". . . in the way the Brontës appear to us today [there is evident] the unquestionable supremacy of Emily." *WH* has "a perfect coherence of purpose."

B21 Adams, Norman O. W., Jr "Byron and the Early Victorians: A Study of His Poetic Influence (1824–1855)" *Dissertation Abstracts* 16 No 2 (1956) 336–337
   EB is one of the minor poets discussed in this study of the nature and extent of Byron's influence. For the minor poets Byron's influence was negative in value: the two themes most used were the Byronic hero, and passion and sentiment.

B22 Adams, Ruth M. "*Wuthering Heights*: The Land East of Eden" *NCF* 13 (June 1958) 58–62
   Reverend Jabes Banderham's [sic] sermon on "Seventy Times Seven" establishes the fact that "no conventional morality prevails" in *WH*. Like Cain and his descendants, these people live outside God's law. The text for the sermon is Genesis 4 (see B293). Reprinted: A104.

B23 Adelman, Seymour "The First American Edition of the Brontës' Poems" *Book Collector* 9 (Summer 1960) 201
   The writer comments (in answer to a query in a previous issue, B162) upon locations of first editions of the *Poems by Currer, Ellis, and Acton Bell*, and describes them. See also B269.

B24 Aiken, Ralph "Wild-heart; An Appreciation of Emily Jane Brontë" *South Atlantic Quarterly* 34 (Apr 1935) 202–210
   EB's Celtic nature impelled her to love sadness. She "gloried in the turbulent" and did not know fear, but she was not morbid. The only thing enigmatic about her was her genius.

B25 Allen, H. Merian "Emily Brontë — One Hundred Years After" *Education* 39 (Dec 1918) 225–230
   The Brontë story, as it is retold here, depicts a loveless and lonely childhood out of which the growth of *WH* was natural. EB is compared to Edgar Allan Poe and *WH* to "The Fall of the House of Usher."

B26 Allott, Miriam "Mrs. Gaskell's 'The Old Nurse's Story': A Link Between *Wuthering Heights* and *The Turn of the Screw*" *Notes and Queries* n s 8 (Mar 1961) 101–102
   Mrs Gaskell's story in the 1852 Christmas number of Dickens' periodical, *Household Words*, was written two years after she read *WH*, is similar to it, and in turn inspired Henry James' *The Turn of the Screw*.

B27 —— "*Wuthering Heights*: The Rejection of Heathcliff?" *Essays in Criticism* 8 (Jan 1958) 27–47
   The author agrees with David Cecil about the storm and calm in *WH* (see A22), but she says this theme is more logical than he pictures it. EB translates the storm elements in the first half of *WH* into calmer, more humanized elements in the second half. EB also takes the calm to a "demoralizing extreme" in Linton Heathcliff, but there is no calm at the end of the story. EB does not answer her question; she only poses it. Partially reprinted: A139a.

B28 Andrews, W. L. [Letter to the Editor] "The Haworth Moors" *The Spectator* 190 (May 29 1953) 702
   The writer disagrees with B. Scholfield (see B289) regarding the modernity of Haworth at the time the Brontës lived there.

B29 —— [Letter to the Editor] "The Miraculous Parsonage" *TLS* (July 31 1948) 429

Mr Andrews takes issue with a statement in a book review that the Brontë novels "have escaped even a temporary eclipse," says that "there was a time when few people read them," and refers particularly to *WH*. See B288 for a reply.

B30 —— "Our Greatest Woman" *BST* 10 (1945) 288–289

EB was esteemed by Alexander Woollcott, who recalled that James M. Barrie described her, in an address, as "our greatest woman." Reprinted: A1.

B31 —— "Ups and Downs of Celebrity" *BST* 11 (1947) 81–87

This is a 100-year history of the readers of *WH* and *Jane Eyre*: the English reading public. Reprinted: A1.

B32 Arnold, Helen H. "Americans and the Brontës" *BST* 10 (1940) 12–14

A survey of American reaction to the Brontë novels when they first appeared. *The American Review,* June 1848: "It [WH] ought to be banished from refined society. . . ." Reprinted: A1.

B33 Baillie, J. B. "Religion and the Brontës" *BST* 7 (1927) 59–69

EB's poetry, "the only revelation of her religious life which we possess," is discussed on p 66–68 from a religious angle.

B34 Baker, Donald W. "Themes of Terror in Nineteenth Century English Fiction: The Shift to the Internal" *Dissertation Abstracts* 16 No 1 (1956) 118–119

"The influence of Gothicism . . . is particularly discernible in Scott, Bulwer-Lytton, the Brontë sisters, Dickens, Collins, and Le Fanu." Terror-fiction, employing psychopathological materials treated subjectively, was written late in the century; sadism, masochism, madness, neuroses, and psychoses are depicted by these authors.

B35 Barker, Ernest "The Inspiration of Emily Brontë" *BST* 12 (1951) 3–9

A discussion of "inspiration" in two senses — that which EB had, and that which she gave others. The three elements of her own inspiration are her Celtic blood, her Yorkshire environment, and — the least fortunate of the three — her mental diet and the books she read.

B36 Barrow, Marjorie Stuart [Letter to the Editor] "Emily Brontë Mysteries" *Poetry Review* 34 (Jan 1943) 59–60

Since Branwell Brontë had a studio in Bradford, the town could have played a part in EB's love life. EB could have visited there, and in this connection "L. Parensell" is mentioned. (See Item B125 for a reply.)

B37 Beblington, W. G. "Haworth Parsonage" *National Review* 123 (July 1944) 77–78

A visit to Haworth reveals the great change and modernization of the area. The threat of bombing caused the Bonnell Collection to be locked away in the musty Brontë Museum.

B37a Beeton, D. R. "Emily Brontë and Jan Christiaan Smuts" *BST* 15 (1968) 214–220

A comparison of an aspect of Field Marshal Smuts' philosophy, as it is expressed in his writings and speeches, with EB's philosophy as it is expressed in her poems and *WH*. (He had praised Olive Schreiner for being like EB.)

B38 Bell, Vereen M. "Character and Point of View in Representative Victorian Novels" *Dissertation Abstracts* 20 (Mar 1960) 3740–3741

EB is one of six novelists treated in this study of the "introspective method of presenting character." ". . . they create an illusion of character . . . that we can be intellectually aware of, but not one that our senses can know."

B39 —— "*Wuthering Heights* and the Unforgiveable Sin" *NCF* 17 (Sept 1962) 188–191

The author repudiates a theory put forth by Shannon (see B293) that the "First of the Seventy-first" sin is that of Catherine's marrying Edgar and traces in *WH* the "absence of for-giveness" theme, as seen in Lockwood's first dream.

B40 —— *"Wuthering Heights* as Epos" *College English* 25 (Dec 1963) 199–208

The mode of double narration was the most expedient way of solving EB's problem of com-munication in *WH*. EB was affected by the oral tradition in her family: her father and her aunt told old Irish tales. EB, using Nelly Dean for the point of view and oral narrative as the medium, could "give full expression to her limited creative gift."

B41 Benson, E. F. "The Brontës" *The Spectator* 146 (Feb 7 1931) 178–179

The author discusses the early misunderstanding of *WH* by the critics, by the public, and by Charlotte Brontë especially.

B42 Bentley, Phyllis [Letter to the Editor] "The Brontës and Methodism" *TLS* (May 20 1949) 329

The aspect of the influence of Methodism upon the Brontës sheds new light on their lives and works. Reprinted: B44.

B43 —— [Letter to the Editor] "The Brontës and Methodism" *TLS* (June 10 1949) 381

The author presents evidence from the childhood plays that the Brontës in their childhood rebelled against Methodism. (See B157 for a reply.)

B44 —— "Dr. Phyllis Bentley on the Brontës and Methodism" *BST* 11 (1949) 270

This is a reprinting of Item B42.

B45 —— "New Brontë Devoirs" *BST* 12 (1955) 361–385

A French exercise written by EB (p 384–385) entitled "Letter" and corrected by M Heger is translated by the author, with the French original printed on the opposite page.

B46 —— "A Novelist Looks at the Brontë Novels" *BST* 11 (1948) 139–151

The Brontë novels are discussed as novels in the light of (1) "kind . . . and (2) degree of impression they make. . . ." which are the criteria by which to judge whether or not they are masterpieces (*WH*, p 147–149).

B47 —— "The Significance of Haworth" *The Trollopian* 2 (Dec 1947) 127–136

This is an expansion of a chapter in her book, *The Brontës* (A10). The Haworth factor (landscape and ideology) supplied half the Brontë "mental equipment with which they molded these materials into art." Their Celtic heredity provided the other half. This is a thorough article on the background of the Brontë family.

B48 Bloomfield, Paul "To Breathe Lightning" *Time and Tide* 29 (Mar 20 1948) 304

A modern book review of *WH*, written in a popular vein. Why do critics discuss what is meant by "Emily Brontë's poetical quality" in *WH* when Heathcliff is the central character? *WH* is seen in terms of "the personal struggle against possession by self-will — Heathcliff's struggle, . . ." and the author touches upon the social implications of this conflict.

B49 Bracco, Edgar Jean "Emily Brontë's Second Novel" *BST* 15 (1966) 29–33

In addition to Newby's letter, there is further evidence in favor of the existence of a second novel written by EB: Charlotte Brontë in one letter refers to "his second work" (Ellis Bell's), and in another she says EB is "too ill to occupy herself with writing."

B50 Bradby, G. F. "Emily Brontë" *Nineteenth Century* 108 (Oct 1930) 533–540

EB's poetry is compared with Shelley's. From her poetry, two characteristics of her person-ality can be derived: a sense of loneliness and a craving for some absorbing kind of love. Reprinted: A16.

B51 Bradner, Leicester "The Growth of *Wuthering Heights*" *PMLA* 48 (Mar 1933) 129–146
One of the best and most comprehensive on the subject, this article explores sources of *WH* and influences on EB with regard to the novel, and includes a full consideration of sources mentioned by critics in the past. The development of EB's poems is traced with reference to the development of *WH*, because the poems were precursory to the novel. Wordsworth's possible influence on EB's poetry (through her childhood reading) is also discussed. Reprinted: A53.

B52 Brash, W. Bardsley "The Brontës of Haworth — Through Trials to Triumph" *London Quarterly and Holborn Review* 167 (Jan 1942) 57–66
An emotional retelling of the Brontë sisters' story, this article centers upon Charlotte Brontë, but the sisters are said to be "a triple cord which cannot be broken."

B53 —— "Emily Brontë" *London Quarterly and Holborn Review* 160 (Oct 1935) 521–523
This review of EB's life refers to G. Elsie Harrison's connection of *WH* with William Grimshaw, the fanatical Methodist. Jabez Bunting, a Wesleyan preacher, is Jabes Branderham in the novel, and William Grimshaw is Mr Earnshaw.

B54 Brick, Allan R. "Lewes's Review of *Wuthering Heights*" *NCF* 14 (Mar 1960) 355–359
An account of George Henry Lewes' 1850 Preface to *WH*, which was the first instance of an eminent critic's granting "the strange novel, which revolted many, its due regard," and of other nineteenth-century criticism of *WH*.

B55 —— "*Wuthering Heights*: Narrators, Audience, and Message" *College English* 21 (Nov 1959) 80–86
"Emily Brontë's narrative form is deeply interfused with her essential message," in *WH*. The novel is compared with Coleridge's *Rime of the Ancient Mariner* wherein the wedding guest is the "personified audience" as is Lockwood in *WH*. Reprinted: A104.

B56 Brown, Helen [Letter to the Editor] "Emily Brontë's Poems" *TLS* (Dec 21 1951) 821
The writer comments on "The Visionary" and EB's poems in general.

B57 —— "The Influence of Byron on Emily Brontë" *Modern Language Review* 34 (July 1939) 374–381
EB's poetry has "resemblances of mood, and [of] the cadence and movement of the verse" to Byron's. The Byron influence would also explain her "tragic imaginings."

B58 ——, and Joan Mott "The Gondal Saga" *BST* 9 (1938) 155–172
This is the first construction of EB's poems in an effort to find a continuous story in them. It precedes F. E. Ratchford's *Gondal's Queen* (see A149) and differs from her interpretation in pointing out three heroines instead of one.

B59 —— "The Gondal Saga: Unpublished Verses by Emily Brontë" *TLS* (Feb 19 1938) 121. (See also *TLS* [Mar 19 1938] 188, which contains a slight correction of this article.)
The two unpublished poems are in the notebook entitled by EB "Gondal," which was presented to the British Museum in 1933. Although the other poems in it were previously published, this manuscript brought to light a considerable number of differences from the published versions.

B60 Brown, T. J. "English Literary Autographs, XVII: The Brontës" *Book Collector* 5 (Spring 1956) 55–56
All four Brontës had a "microscopic" handwriting as well as a normal handwriting. This article gives the manuscript sources of both handwritings for each Brontë, describes them, and includes facsimiles (8) of a sample of each handwriting.

B61 Buchen, Irving H. "Emily Brontë and the Metaphysics of Childhood and Love" *NCF* 22 (June 1967) 63–70
This is an excellent study of EB's metaphysics. Its purpose is "to read the poems in their own light and then to read the novel in the light of the poems." The love experience is related to childhood: "the second birth and death is that of love. . . ." *WH* is a story of childhood, and "paradise lost and regained" for the child and for the soul. Reprinted: A194a.

B62 —— "Metaphysical and Social Evolution in *Wuthering Heights*" *Victorian Newsletter* 31 (Spring 1967) 15–20
There seem to be gaps between EB's "poetry and fiction, her metaphysics [See J. H. Miller, A125, which Buchen footnotes here] and sociology, and the two love stories in the novel." EB does integrate these, however, as the author points out.

B63 Buckler, William E. "Chapter VII of *Wuthering Heights*: A Key to Interpretation" *NCF* 7 (June 1952) 51–55
This chapter is a key to understanding the novel because in it Heathcliff's isolation becomes complete, Catherine sets her course, and the trustworthiness of Nelly Dean as a narrator is established.

B64 Buckley, Vincent "Passion and Control in *Wuthering Heights*" *Southern Review: An Australian Journal of Literary Studies* 1 (1964) 5–23
The first half of this article is a careful and thorough investigation of the prose of *WH* and the controlled effects which are made stronger by a "commonsense realism." The second half is an excellent and original discussion of the nature of the Catherine-Heathcliff relationship in which the author rejects the widely-held idea that sexuality does not have a part in it. Partially reprinted: A139a.

B65 Bullock, F. A. "The Genius of Emily Brontë" *BST* 9 (1937) 115–128
The writings of EB should be treated objectively, not subjected to psychoanalysis. Her quality of imagination is "an instrument and vehicle of knowledge . . . it tells us about the structure of reality," and should not be used to tell us about EB herself.

B66 Butterfield, Herbert "Charlotte Brontë and Her Sisters in the Crucial Year" *BST* 14 (1963) 3–17
This is a modern evaluation of the Brontë's development toward literary careers. The crucial year was 1845 when the Brontë children came together again after being separated from each other and Haworth. From the dates of her poems, EB's creative period began in 1844.

B67 Carr, D. R. W. "The Sphinx of English Poetry" *Poetry Review* 34 (Mar – Apr 1943) 85–90
Personally, EB shared with Emily Dickinson an unconcern about publishing what she wrote and about a posthumous fame. EB's poems reflect her self-containment and mysticism. Among those her work has influenced are D. H. Lawrence and Charles Morgan.

B68 Cautley, C. Holmes "Old Haworth Folk Who Knew the Brontës" *Cornhill Magazine* 29 (July 1910) 76–84
This is a record of conversations with the few people in Haworth who remembered the Brontës.

B69 Chadwick, Esther Alice "Emily Brontë" *Nineteenth Century* 86 (Oct 1919) 677–687
The author discusses Charlotte Brontë's characterization of EB as Shirley Keeldar in *Shirley*, and what past and present critics have said about EB and her work, in an attempt to depict EB's personality.

B70 —— "The Haworth Parsonage: The Home of the Brontës" *Nineteenth Century* 103 (Jan 1928) 133–144
Haworth Parsonage, which was to be converted into a Brontë Museum in the summer of 1928, was well known before the Brontës made it famous because Reverend William Grimshaw

lived there. There is a description of the parsonage, inside and out, and a discussion of Brontë relics and manuscripts.

Chambers, L. R. *see* B164.

*B70a Champion, Larry S. "Heathcliff: Study in Authorial Technique" *Ball University Forum* 9 (1968) 19–25

B71 Chase, Richard "The Brontës: A Centennial Observance (Reconsiderations VIII)" *Kenyon Review* 9 (Autumn 1947) 487–506
Jane Eyre and *WH* are both considered, and EB's poetry is related to *WH*. These Victorian novels translated the social customs of the time into mythical art, whereas other Victorian novels were more concerned with society per se. "The Brontë novels are concerned with the neuroses of women in a man's society." The Brontë heroes and heroines are centers in an enclosed philosophy like A. J. Toynbee's, which gives a new interpretation to the novels. Reprinted: A104, A25.

B72 Childe, Wilfred R. "The Literary Background of the Brontës" *BST* 10 (1944) 204–208
This article is chiefly evidence that much more is known about Charlotte Brontë's literary background than EB's, although some guesses are made regarding what EB read.

B73 Christian, Mildred G. "A Census of Brontë Manuscripts in the United States" *The Trollopian* 2 (Dec 1947) 177–199 — 3 (Dec 1948) 215–233
Many of the Brontë manuscripts are in the United States, and this is a "finding list" as well as a history of the manuscripts. They are arranged chronologically by date and separated as to author. *The Trollopian* 2 (Mar 1948) contains "Manuscripts of Poems by Emily Brontë" on p 243–253.

B74 —— "III. A Guide to Research Materials on the Major Victorians (Part II): The Brontës" *Victorian Newsletter* 13 (Spring 1958) 19
This is a listing and discussion of the Brontë manuscript material available to students in the United States and in England. The author notes that no definitive bibliography of works of the Brontës yet exists.

B75 Clay, Charles T. "Notes on the Chronology of *Wuthering Heights*" *BST* 12 (1952) 100–105
An excellent, fully-documented analysis of the intricate chronology of *WH* with a genealogical table of the Earnshaw and Linton families. The genealogical table differs slightly from C. P. Sanger's table (see A166) in his *The Structure of* Wuthering Heights.

B76 Collins, Clifford "Theme and Conventions in *Wuthering Heights*" *The Critic* 1 (Autumn 1947) 43–50
Catherine and Heathcliff's love is a life-force relationship, and is a principle because the relationship is of an ideal nature. The author touches on a comparison with D. H. Lawrence. Reprinted: A165.

B77 Cook, Davidson "Brontë Manuscripts in the Law Collection" *The Bookman* (London) 69 (Nov 1925) 100–104
The collection contains manuscripts of EB's poems and the manuscript of the 1841 "diary."

B78 —— "Emily Brontë's Poems" *Nineteenth Century* 100 (Aug 1926) 248–262
Textual corrections of EB's poems and her unpublished poems are printed in this article for the first time. Especially interesting is EB's original poem printed alongside the poem as edited by Charlotte Brontë.

B79 Cooper, Dorothy J. "The Romantics and Emily Brontë" *BST* 12 (1952) 106–112
EB's similarity to the Romantics lies in her appreciation of the individual. She is compared with Keats, Shelley, Byron, Coleridge, Wordsworth, and others.

B80 Copley, J. *"Wuthering Heights* and *Shirley* — A Parallel" *Notes and Queries* n s 3 (Nov 1956) 499–500

The endings of the two novels are similar in their reference to ghosts. The author suggests that Charlotte Brontë in *Shirley* is "reaching out half-heartedly to the world of *Wuthering Heights.*"

B81 Cornish, Dorothy H. "The Brontës' Study of French" *BST* 11 (1947) 97–100

Two of EB's French compositions are translated by the author: "Portrait: Harold the Night before Hastings," and "Filial Love." (See A152, B15 and B193 or B194 for other essays by EB.)

B82 Cott, Jeremy "Structures of Sound: The Last Sentence of *Wuthering Heights*" *Texas Studies in Literature and Language* 6 (Summer 1964) 280–289

This is an excellent linguistic analysis of the structural grammar in the last sentence of *WH*, relating it to EB's poetic sensibility.

*B82a Cowhig, Ruth M. *"Wuthering Heights* — An Amoral Book?" *Use of English* 17 (Winter 1965) 123–126

*B83 Craig, J. M. [A discussion of the legal problem in *WH*] *Saturday Westminster Gazette* (Sept 9 1916)

B84 Crandall, Norma "Charlotte, Emily and Branwell Brontë" *American Book Collector* 13 (Feb 1963) 21–22

The Brontës' "eccentric childhood produced odd lives and neurotic personalities," but "psychological disability in combination with innate gifts is a likely, fertile field for real and marvelous achievement."

B85 Cunliffe, W. R. "The Brontës in Other People's Books" *BST* 11 (1950) 332–336

The Brontës are referred to in James Hilton's *Lost Horizon*, in Dorothy Sayer's *Gaudy Night*, and in other books.

B86 —— "Emily Brontë: A Clue to Her Appearance" *BST* 13 (1959) 363

Charlotte Brontë, in a letter, describes EB's resemblance to George Henry Lewes. A pencil sketch of Lewes is in this issue of *BST*.

B87 Curtis, Myra "Cowan Bridge School: An Old Prospectus Re-examined" *BST* 12 (1953) 187–192

EB entered this school in November 1824. The authenticity of the old prospectus manuscript used by some Brontë biographers is questioned, and documents known to be genuine are reprinted here.

B88 —— "The 'Profile' Portrait" *BST* 13 (1959) 342–346

This is a discussion about whether this portrait is of Emily Brontë or Anne Brontë, with the conclusion that it is Anne.

Day-Lewis, C. *see* B202.

B89 Dean, Christopher "Joseph's Speech in *Wuthering Heights*" *Notes and Queries* n s 7 (Feb 1960) 73–76

The author examines the accuracy and consistency of the West Riding dialect as it is written in Joseph's speech in *WH*. Although it is judged not entirely scientifically accurate, EB achieved her literary purpose of creating a local atmosphere.

B90 De Selincourt, Ernest "The Genius of the Brontës" *BST* 2 (Jan 1906) 234–255

The novels of Charlotte Brontë and EB are considered together. They are distinct from other nineteenth-century novels because "whatever their theme, we never get far away from their haunting presence." The novels have a poetic atmosphere. The Brontës are compared with Jane Austen.

B91 Devlin, James E. *"Wuthering Heights*: The Dominant Image" *Discourse; A Review of the Liberal Arts* 5 (Summer 1962) 337–346
This essay shows very capably that "the motif of the novel, the frustration of psychic forces, is buttressed by a complex and skillful imagery which reflects . . . the main theme." For instance, action in *WH* is generated when a character moves from one house to the other because the houses represent two worlds. There is also a "thick web of imagery of restraint" throughout the novel.

B92 Dickinson, A. "Spell of the Brontës" *London Quarterly and Holborn Review* 143 (Apr 1925) 256–259
The author's parents and their friends could remember the Brontë family, but knew surprisingly little about them. Here are accounts of some conversations with those who knew the Brontës.

B93 Dickson, Sarah Augusta "The Arents Collection of Books in Parts and Associated Literature" *Bulletin of The New York Public Library* 61 (June 1957) 267–280 [274]
The Brontë sisters are mentioned briefly, but none of the Brontë works is included in this collection.

B94 Dingle, Herbert "An Examination of Emily Brontë's Poetry from an Unaccustomed Angle" *BST* 14 (1964) 5–10
Permeating EB's poetry are references to the weather, the time of day, the time of year, and the light. Correlating the weather records of the Haworth area (the weather record accompanies this issue) with the dates of her poems may be one yet-unexplored method of determining which poems are Gondal (in which the Haworth weather probably would not figure) and which are personal.

B95 Dobson, Mildred A. [Letter to the Editor] "Emily Brontë" *TLS* (Aug 24 1948) 471
Partly in answer to A. B. Hughes (see B178), the author refers to her article in *BST* (see B96) regarding the definition of "mystic" as it applies to EB.

B96 —— "Was Emily Brontë a Mystic?" *BST* 11 (1948) 166–175
A definition of "mystic" is given and it is pointed out that there is insufficient autobiographical evidence to answer the question. There is, however, an exploration of EB's possible mystic experience as reflected in her poems (see B95 and B178).

B97 Dodds, Madeleine Hope "George Hudson and the Brontës" *BST* 14 (1962) 36–37
Miss Branwell left her capital to the three Brontë sisters and a cousin. "On the initiative of Emily Brontë she and her sisters invested the capital . . . in the York and North Midland Railway." George Hudson owned the railroad.

B98 —— "The Gondal Poems and Emily Brontë" *Notes and Queries* 188 (May 5 1945) 189
This short article is in reference to poem fragments of EB's and Robert Bridges' interpretation of them (A18). The poems concerned are "Tell Me, Tell Me, Smiling Child" and "The Inspiring Music's Thrilling Sound," and they are related to Gondal.

B99 —— "Gondaliand" *Modern Language Review* 18 (Jan 1923) 9–21
This is the first published attempt to connect EB's poems with her childhood Gondal chronicle. Both the chronicle and the poems contributed to her literary powers shown in *WH*.

B100 —— "Heathcliff's Country" *Modern Language Review* 39 (Apr 1944) 116–129

Heathcliff's mysterious home, from which he came as a child and to which he returned to become wealthy, is not accounted for by the author's desire to avoid explanations, but was derived from Gondal. In this discussion of Gondal, the author differs with F. E. Ratchford's construction of the Gondal epic (see A148, *The Brontës' Web of Childhood*): there is no single dominating character in the story.

B101 —— "A Second Visit to Gondaliand" *Modern Language Review* 21 (Oct 1926) 373–379

"The Twelve Adventurers," recently published by C. Shorter and C. W. Hatfield, contains stories written by Charlotte Brontë between the ages of 12 and 21. These stories are shown to be closely connected with EB's poems.

B101a —— "A Second Visit to Gondaliand" *Modern Language Review* 22 (Apr 1927) 197–198

A corrective note to her previous article (B101) taking into account the 1923 edition of *The Complete Poems of Emily Jane Brontë* and discussing changes of authorship of some of the poems.

*B102 Doheny, John "From PMLA to *Wuthering Heights*" *Paunch* 21 (Oct 1964) 21–34

A criticism of Wade Thompson's article "Infanticide and Sadism in *Wuthering Heights*" (see B307). [From an abstract in *Abstracts of English Studies*.]

B103 Dooley, Lucile "Psychoanalysis of the Character and Genius of Emily Brontë" *Psychoanalytic Review* 17 (Apr 1930) 208–239

This is a very interesting psychological evaluation of EB's character. A closed family circle, such as the Brontës had, "intensifies family relations and conserves emotions of infancy." EB's idea of "the doomed child" (her feeling about herself) is expressed in her poems and in *WH*. Nature was her "adopted mother," and her love of liberty came from her rebellion against her father. Reprinted: A45.

B104 Doyle, Louis F. "Of Something That Is Gone" *America* 77 (June 14 1947) 297–298

EB's inexperience with the world enabled her to write a masterpiece, *WH*. Modern writers cannot imitate her because they will not melt their experience and imagination down "in the crucible of the creative faculty until it is workable. . . ."

B105 Drew, Arnold P. "Emily Brontë and *Hamlet*" *Notes and Queries* n s 1 (Feb 1954) 81–82

Catherine Linton's mad scene, and her words while she is pulling feathers from her pillow, are compared to Ophelia's flower speech in *Hamlet*, which the author suggests served as a model for Catherine's speech.

B105a Drew, David P. "Emily Brontë and Emily Dickinson as Mystic Poets" *BST* 15 (1968) 227–232

There are parallels between these two poets in character, environment and poetry, but this article takes up in detail a common theme in their poetry: the expression of the mystical experience.

B106 Drew, Philip "Charlotte Brontë as a Critic of *Wuthering Heights*" *NCF* 18 (Mar 1964) 365–381

In her 1850 preface, Charlotte Brontë correctly evaluated the characters in *WH*: Nelly Dean is a moral force, and Heathcliff an evil force with whom we can sympathize as he works out his doom but whom we cannot call a hero. Reprinted: A53.

B107 Dugas, Joseph Henry "The Literary Reputation of the Brontës: 1846–1951" *Dissertation Abstracts* 12 No 1 (1952) 61–62

This very thorough dissertation is "an attempt to describe and analyze the fame of the fiction written by Charlotte and Emily Brontë." As understanding of prose fiction grew, so did the popularity of *WH*. Although *Jane Eyre* was the more popular novel in the 1850s, *WH* is more popular in the 1950s. This dissertation has a 27-page bibliography.

B108 Durrell, Lawrence "Dylan Thomas and Emily Bronte: The Only Woman I've Ever Loved" *BST* 14 (1963) 36
This is a reprinting of Item A50.

B109 Edgar, Pelham "Judgments on Appeal: II. The Brontës" *Queen's Quarterly* 39 (Aug 1932) 414–422
EB and *WH* are discussed on p 418–422. There should be a detachment between a work of art and the personal life of the author. The writer says of *WH*: the character Nelly Dean's narration of the impassioned story is a formal flaw which the book survives. Her role is unbelievable, and there is a break in interest when the first Catherine dies. Reprinted: A51.

B110 Edgerley, C. Mabel "The Brontë Struggle against Illness" *BST* 10 (1944) 231–233
A description of the Brontës' illnesses and deaths, partly supported by data on the death certificates.

*B111 —— "Causes of Death of the Brontës" *British Medical Journal* [pre 1934]
This article contains the certified cause of death of EB. Reprinted: A1, B112.

B112 —— "Causes of Death of the Brontës" *BST* (1934) 139–142
This is a reprinting of Item B111.

B113 —— "Emily Brontë: A National Portrait Vindicated" *BST* 8 (1932) 27–32
The authenticity of EB's portrait in the National Portrait Gallery, London, is discussed.

B114 —— "Ponden Hall and the Heatons" *BST* 10 (1945) 265–268
There is a possibility that the house, Ponden Hall, and the Heaton family were related to the setting of *WH* because EB visited there.

B115 —— "The Structure of Haworth Parsonage" *BST* 9 (1936) 27–31
A description of the Parsonage accompanied by an architect's drawing of the floor plan and elevations.

B116 —— "Tabitha Ackroyd" *BST* 10 (1941) 62–68
This is an account of "Tabby," the elderly woman who lived with the Brontës. She took care of the house and the children from 1824 until just before her death in 1855.

B117 Edwards, R. A. [Letter to the Editor] "Pot-Shooting" *TLS* (May 6 1949) 297
He comments on the article "Pot-Shooting" (B13), emphasizing that the Brontës did not only "know" Methodism; they were "soaked in it."

B118 Egan, Eileen M. "The Brontës and Catholicism" *The Magnificat* 91 (Feb 1953) 203–205
This is a discussion, from a sectarian point of view, of the reasons why the Brontës were not Catholic.

B119 Elliott, W. Thompson "Atmosphere in the Bronte Works" *BST* 7 (1928) 119–136 [120–131]
EB's personality is seen as mystic, and the setting, characters, and story of *WH* as belonging to another world.

B120 Evans, Margiad "Byron and Emily Brontë: An Essay" *Life and Letters* 57 (June 1948) 193–216
Byron, like EB, was a mystic — especially near the time of his death. This is a comparison of their poetry, their philosophies, their diction, and their religions. *Manfred* is compared with *WH*; *Manfred* is a Heathcliff with more humanity.

B121 Fenton, Edith M. "The Spirit of Emily Brontë's *Wuthering Heights* as Distinguished from That of Gothic Romance" *Washington University Studies* 8 (Humanistic Series) (1920) 103–122
This is a thorough study of the elements of similarity in *WH* and Gothic Romance. The dreams in *WH* are discussed in terms of Freudian theory.

B122 Field, W. T. "Catalogue of Objects in the Museum of the Brontë Society" *BST* 4 (June 1908) 43–72
Two items listed in the catalogue — a water color by EB and the printed circular for the Brontë sisters' proposed school — are both also reproduced.

B123 Fielding, K. J. "The Brontës and 'The North American Review': A Critic's Strange Guesses" *BST* 13 (1956) 14–18
The review (Oct 1848) of *Jane Eyre, WH,* and *The Tenant of Wildfell Hall* is reprinted here and contrasted with Charlotte Brontë's letter in which she describes her sisters' reactions as she read it to them.

B123a Fike, Francis "Bitter Herbs and Wholesome Medicines: Love as Theological Affirmation in *Wuthering Heights*" *NCF* 23 (Sept 1968) 127–149
The theological affirmation derives from the qualities of love portrayed in *WH*. The central Christian reality, as EB saw it, moves out of the lives of the nominally or neurotically religious characters into the keeping of those — Catherine and Heathcliff, and Cathy and Hareton — who embody Christian reality in their lives.

B124 Flahiff, Frederick T. C. "Formative Ideas in the Novels of Charlotte and Emily Jane Brontë" *Dissertation Abstracts* 27 (Sept 1966) 746A–747A
The second part of this thesis deals with EB and problems arising out of *WH*. EB resolved in her one novel many technical problems with which Charlotte Brontë struggled. *WH*'s narrative structure "balances involvement against detachment." *WH* is compared and contrasted to Charlotte's novels; *WH* is not like Charlotte's novels but has more affinity with *King Lear*.

B125 Fleming, Edward V. [Letter to the Editor] "Emily Brontë and 'Louis Parensell'" *Poetry Review* 34 (May – June 1943) 190
This is a brief account of the "Louis Parensell-Love's Farewell" discovery, in reply to Item B36.

B126 Ford, Boris *"Wuthering Heights" Scrutiny* 7 (Mar 1939) 375–389
"By common consent there is something wrong with *Wuthering Heights* . . . ," but it has "rigid control and a clarity of execution that are truly remarkable." The texture of the prose is investigated, and the two themes (Catherine-Heathcliff and Catherine-Hareton) are traced and explicated. To be thought "terrible" and not "enjoyable" *WH* has to be stubbornly misread. Partially reprinted: A139a.

B127 Fotheringham, James "The Work of Emily Brontë and the Brontë Problem" *BST* 2 (June 1900) 107–134
EB's character is closely bound with *WH*. Her poems are discussed as they pertain to her character and genius. After presenting a critical history of *WH*, the author writes: "It has faults of style, defects of construction. One fault is its double narrative; another is its narration by Nelly Dean. The theme is harsh. "It is a work that can never be popular . . . but it is a work of unquestionable depth, originality, and power, both in conception and execution." The "problem" of the title refers to sources for *WH*, which the author states are Yorkshire, EB's imagination, and the deterioration of Branwell Brontë.

B128 Frank, Maude M. "At the Misses Brontës' Establishment" *Cornhill Magazine* 70 (Feb 1931) 151–168
This article is written in the form of an imaginary drama in which the Brontë sisters are operating the school they never succeeded in establishing.

B129 Fraser, J. "The Name of Action: Nelly Dean and *Wuthering Heights*" *NCF*
20 (Dec 1965) 223–236
Nelly Dean's conduct throughout *WH* is not only justified, but praised. "[Other] critical
attacks [on *WH*] . . . seem to me symptomatic of a too-common sentimentality about wicked-
ness. . . ."

B130 Friesner, Donald N. "Ellis Bell and Israfel" *BST* 14 (1964) 11–18
This is a comparison of the lives and the poems of EB and Edgar Allan Poe.

B131 Fulcher, Paul M. [Letter to the Editor] "Emily Brontë" *Saturday Review of
Literature* 5 (Sept 22 1928) 150
A brief comment called forth by a review of Romer Wilson's biography (see A212) of EB.
He criticizes the reviewer's conjecturing because it is like that of Romer Wilson.

B132 Garbett, Cyril "The Courage of the Brontës" *BST* 11 (1950) 327–331
This is a sermon preached at Haworth Parish Church on May 28 1950. "Their [the
Brontës'] tragedy should shame those who . . . complain over smaller sorrows."

B133 Gérin, Winifred "Byron's Influence on the Brontës" *Keats-Shelley Memorial
Bulletin* 17 (1966) 1–19
(The frontispiece in this issue is "a water-colour by Emily Brontë of Lady Harley.") Four
general characteristics of Byron's poetry are particularized and they sound remarkably like
WH and *Jane Eyre*. *WH* and EB's poems are discussed on p 11–17. That Heathcliff is a very
Byronic hero is shown by a comparison with Manfred.

B134 Gilbert, Ariadne "Children of the Moors" *St. Nicholas* 43 (May 1916) 646–
650
A short informal history of the Brontës, containing a great deal of supposition about their
personalities. EB's homesickness is related to one of her poems.

B135 Girdler, Lew "*Wuthering Heights* and Shakespeare" *Huntington Library
Quarterly* 19 (Aug 1956) 385–392
EB was "so imbued with [Shakespeare's] plays that words and phrases from them sprang
readily to her mind and often colored her writing." At two points in *WH*, EB refers directly to
Shakespeare: to *Twelfth Night* and *King Lear*. These are the only evidences from her own pen
that she knew Shakespeare. However, a comparison of *WH* with the plays Charlotte Brontë
recommends in a letter to Ellen Nussey shows "striking parallels in theme, characterization,
structure, and literary devices. . . ." The plays considered are *Hamlet, Macbeth, Richard III,
King Lear*, and *Taming of the Shrew*.

B136 Gleckner, Robert F. "Time in *Wuthering Heights*" *Criticism* 1 (Fall 1959)
328–338
This is a perceptive essay by a student of William Blake. The time theme, central to *WH*,
alone accounts for the character of Heathcliff. The past increasingly presses upon the present
in the narrative and in Heathcliff's mind. The key temporal images are the window and the
mirror.

B137 Goldstone, Herbert "*Wuthering Heights* Revisited" *English Journal* 48
(Apr 1959) 175–185
WH is now widely read and taught in senior high schools. This article, directed to high
school teachers, rejects the analyses of *WH* by David Cecil (A22) and Dorothy Van Ghent
(A192) and asserts that "the view of life in the book is direct, simple, very comprehensive,
and clearly presented."

B138 Gordan, John D. "What's in a Name? Authors and Their Pseudonyms" *Bulletin of The New York Public Library* 60 (Mar 1956) 107–128 [109]
The subtitle is "Notes on an Exhibition from the Berg Collection." *Poems by Currer, Ellis,
and Acton Bell* is included in this list of pseudonymous books. The real names of the authors
are withheld until the end of the article.

B139 Gose, Elliott B., Jr "*Wuthering Heights*: The Heath and the Hearth" *NCF* 21 (June 1966) 1–19

WH is seen on four levels: fairy tale, religion and the Bible, traditional elements of nature, and the process of initiation. Fire imagery is discussed. The "hearth" is synonymous with weak characters, i.e., the Lintons, and the "heath" with the strong characters, i.e., Heathcliff.

B140 Gosse, Edmund "The Challenge of the Brontës" *BST* 2 (Feb 1904) 195–202

Although the focus is upon Charlotte Brontë and EB is generally included in statements about "the Brontë sisters," the article points out that pride, stubbornness, and imperviousness to public opinion were characteristics shared by the sisters. Reprinted: A66, A67.

B141 Green, David Bronte "Portraits of the Brontë Sisters" *The Connoisseur* 120 (Sept 1947) 26–28, 66

The Brontë portraits are discussed, and the opinions of them held by Charlotte Brontë, Mrs Gaskell, and others are reprinted.

*B142 Green, Joseph J. "The Brontë-Wheelwright Friendship" *The Friends Quarterly Examiner* (Jan 1916)

B143 Greenwood, J. F. "Haworth" *BST* 2 (May 1901) 151–166

A history and description of Haworth, including quotes from the church registers regarding the Brontës' deaths; the Yorkshire weather and historical events are also included.

B144 Grimshaw, Beatrice "First Love: A Glory That Is Never Forgotten" *John O'London's Weekly* (Oct 4 1924) 4

This sentimental investigation of "first love" includes Charlotte Brontë, Byron, and Keats, among others. EB "knew love," and her poem "Cold in the Earth" is quoted to prove it.

*145 —— "Emily and Charlotte Brontë" *John O'London's Weekly* (Oct 1921)

B146 Grove, Robin "*Wuthering Heights*" *Critical Review* 8 (1965) 71–87

This is an investigation of the bond and relationship between Catherine and Heathcliff which is the "great fact and focus" of *WH*. EB is concerned with the unnaturalness of their love. The Hareton and Catherine Linton love is a kind of anti-masque or counterfeit of that of Catherine and Heathcliff.

*B146a Gutteling, J. F. C. ["Emily Brontë"] *Students' Monthly* (Dec 1918)

B147 Hadow, W. H. "Education, As Treated by the Brontës" *BST* 6 (1925) 261–275

A better title would be "the education received by the Brontës." Cowan Bridge School, Father Brontë (who as a father was not admirable), and the Brontës' reading matter are discussed.

B148 Hafley, James "The Villain in *Wuthering Heights*" *NCF* 13 (Dec 1958) 199–215

Nelly Dean is the villain. Frequently in a position to interfere with the actions of the characters and resentful and ambitious because of her station, Nelly manipulates people and events so that upon Catherine's death she finally becomes mistress of Thrushcross Grange. Reprinted: A104.

B149 Hagan, John "Control of Sympathy in *Wuthering Heights*" *NCF* 21 (Mar 1967) 305–323

This is an analysis of the way in which EB accomplishes and sustains the reader's moral "double view" that allows him to disapprove of the actions of Heathcliff and Catherine, and yet never to lose sympathy with them.

B150 Haldane, Elizabeth S. "The Brontës and Their Biographers" *Nineteenth Century* 112 (Dec 1932) 752–764

The biographers treated here are Mrs Gaskell and E. F. Benson. Various letters to and from people who knew the Brontës are discussed.

B151 Haldane, R. B. "Emily Brontë's Place in Literature" *BST* 2 (May 1901) 142–150

Of the two sisters, Charlotte and Emily, Emily was the poet. "Emily must be placed not only above Charlotte, but with Shakespeare and Milton. . . ."

B152 Haley, William "Three Sisters" *BST* 11 (1947) 73–80

EB, Charlotte Brontë, and Anne Brontë had different personalities; they are compared with Chekov's Olga, Irina, and Masha Prozorov. Reprinted: A1.

B153 Hall, Henry C. "Early Victorian Portrait: Is It Emily Brontë?" *Apollo* 59 (Mar 1954) 68

An unsigned portrait, dated circa 1838–40, is thought possibly to be of EB, but there is no conclusive proof. An illustration of the portrait accompanies the article.

*B154 Hanson, T. W. "Emily Brontë's Footprints" *Municipal Libraries Readers' Guide* (Feb 1910)

B155 —— "The Local Colour of *Wuthering Heights*" *BST* 6 (1924) 201–219

The author is a native of the moorlands of Yorkshire. He relates *WH* and some of EB's poetry to the country and to the climate.

B156 Harbottle, A. [Letter to the Editor] "A Brontë Metre" *TLS* (Nov 26 1938) 755

The same metre that EB uses in "No Coward Soul Is Mine" was used by Dr Monsell in his hymn, "Birds Have Their Quiet Nests." (See also B231.)

B157 Harrison, G. Elsie [Letter to the Editor] "The Brontës and Methodism" *TLS* (June 24 1949) 413

She makes the distinction that she is not, in her book *The Clue to the Brontës* (A76), trying to prove the Brontës Methodists, but is pointing out the enormity of the Methodist influence upon them. (This letter is possibly a reply to Letters to the Editor from P. Bentley [B43] and T. Olsen [B253]).

B158 Hartley, L. P. "Emily Brontë in Gondal and Gaaldine" *BST* 14 (1965) 1–15

WH presents "the dilemma of the soul in the most naked and uncompromising fashion." EB's essay on Harold on the eve of the Battle of Hastings "shows that in certain moods Emily was in love with defeat and possibly with death." Some of her poems are visions of lost happiness. This is a long, well-documented assertion of EB's unhappiness and possibly misanthropy.

—— *see* B164.

B159 Hatfield, C. W. [Letter to the Editor] "Emily Brontë's 'Lost Love'" *TLS* (Aug 29 1936) 697

Mr Hatfield asserts that EB had no "lost love"; the letter is in response to a review of V. Moore's *The Life and Eager Death of Emily Brontë* (A128) entitled "Emily Brontë's 'Lost Love.'"

B160 Hawkes, Jacquetta "Emily Brontë in the Natural Scene" *BST* 12 (1953) 173–186

EB's Celtic inheritance was sufficiently alien to the moors to allow her to respond to them "with heightened force." EB's poetry contrasts dark and light, and the darkness is of the moors.

B161 —— "The Haworth Moors" *Spectator* 190 (May 15 1953) 600

This is a personal description of Haworth and the moors. The contrast between the dark moorland and the light valley is related to EB's poetry and *WH*. (See B289 for a reply.)

B162 Hayward, John [Letter to the Editor] "The First American Edition of the Brontës' Poems" *Book Collector* 8 (Winter 1959) 432
This is a query about the printing and publication of the *Poems by Currer, Ellis, and Acton Bell*. (See B23 and B269 for replies.)

B163 Hedley, Arthur [Letter to the Editor] "Emily Brontë's Second Novel" *TLS* (Sept 6 1947) 451
In one of Charlotte Brontë's letters written in 1848 she states that EB is writing a novel. This letter asks what became of this "second novel."

B164 Henderson, Philip; Edwin Morgan; L. R. Chambers; L. P. Hartley [Letters to the Editor] "Emily Brontë's Poems" *TLS* (1949) (Jan 29) 73; (Feb 12) 110; (Mar 12) 169; (Apr 9) 233; (Apr 23) 270
This is a controversy about EB's poem "The Visionary," as to whether or not Charlotte Brontë wrote the last two verses. The editor put an end to the discussion with his article, "Pot-Shooting" (B13).

B165 Henderson, Philip [Letter to the Editor] "Emily Brontë's Poems" *TLS* (Nov 30 1951) 765
He defends his edition of EB's poems and discusses the question of the authorship of "The Visionary" which has been argued before in *TLS* (B164).

B166 Henneman, John B. "The Brontë Sisters" *Sewanee Review* 9 (Apr 1901) 220–234
The Brontës' environment had more influence upon them than their ancestry. "Tabby," the Yorkshire woman who took care of the Brontë children, gave them insight into Yorkshire human nature and recounted the folklore. They were also strongly influenced by their father.

B167 Hewish, John [Letter to the Editor] "Emily Brontë's Missing Novel" *TLS* (Mar 10 1966) 197
EB did not write a "missing" second novel. Newby, her publisher, referred to *The Tenant of Wildfell Hall* but was careless and mistakenly addressed the envelope to Ellis Bell instead of Acton Bell. (See B197 for a reply.) Reprinted: B168.

B168 —— "Emily Brontë's Second Novel" *BST* 15 (1966) 28
This is a reprinting of Item B167.

—— *see* B267.

B169 Hirst, J. C. "The Burial Place of the Brontës" *BST* 9 (1938) 181–185
The author, Rector of Haworth, gives an exact record of the Brontës' burial place. Reprinted: A1.

B170 Holgate, Ivy "The Branwells at Penzance" *BST* 13 (1960) 425–432
"The Brontë juvenilia . . . abounds in sea-imagery and is set in foreign lands," due to the influence of their aunt, Elizabeth Branwell, who told them stories of Penzance and the sea. The article also gives a record of Branwell property and the family in Penzance.

B171 —— "The Brontës at Thornton: 1815–1820" *BST* 13 (1959) 323–338
Thornton is the birthplace of Charlotte, Branwell, Emily, and Anne Brontë. The Brontës lived there from 1815 to 1820. Inventories of the chapel are listed; the church records and an old diary mention the dates Patrick Brontë preached.

B172 —— "The Structure of *Shirley*" *BST* 14 (1962) 27–35
This article contains a description of EB as the heroine in Charlotte Brontë's novel *Shirley*.

B172a Holloway, Owen E. "*Wuthering Heights*: A Matter of Method" *Northern Miscellany of Literary Criticism* 1 (Autumn 1953) 65–74

The most interesting aspect of *WH* is the unique position it holds in novel literature. Its artistic strength lies in the method of narration: the protagonists are hardly presented directly at all. Since the story is not chronologically straightforward, the reader must participate and build the story for himself. The present is the appearance of things; that which is narrated of the past is the reality; and when reality has filled appearance, there is another great change to a new reality of the future.

B173 Hopewell, Donald "Cowan Bridge" *BST* 6 (1921) 43–49
This is an illustrated description of the school and the records of the school concerning the Brontës.

B174 —— "The Misses Brontë — Victorians" *BST* 10 (1940) 3–11
The author discusses the extent to which the three Brontë sisters are "Victorian." *WH* is the only "perfectly constructed" Brontë novel. Reprinted: A1.

B175 —— "A Westminster Abbey Memorial to the Brontës" *BST* 9 (1939) 236–238
The inscription on the Memorial (to be placed in The Poets' Corner) uses the last line of EB's poem "Old Stoic": ". . . with courage to endure."

B176 House, Roy T. "Emily Brontë" *The Nation* 107 (Aug 17 1918) 169–170
August 20 1918 would have been EB's 100th birthday. "*Wuthering Heights* is nearly forgotten by the general public, while *Jane Eyre* . . . is still . . . widely read." He praises EB as the "poet turned novelist."

B177 Howells, William Dean "Heroines of Nineteenth-Century Fiction. XIX: The Two Catherines of Emily Brontë" *Harper's Bazaar* 33 (Dec 29 1900) 2224–2230
WH is compared, in some respects, with *Jane Eyre*. "Seldom has a great romance been worse contrived," he says, referring to the double narrative. However, he praises EB's non-intrusive authorship, and the "unfaltering truth of her scenes." Reprinted: A87.

B178 Hughes, A. B. [Letter to the Editor] "Emily Brontë" *TLS* (Aug 7 1948) 443
The writer points out the reasons he believes EB was not a mystic. (See B95 for a reply.)

B179 Huguenin, Charles A. "Brontëana at Princeton University: The Parrish Collection" *BST* 12 (1955) 391–400
The collection contains early editions of the poetry of the three Brontë sisters and early editions of *WH*.

B180 Insh, George P. "Haworth Pilgrimage" *BST* 10 (1944) 209–213
The significance of Heathcliff is found in man's struggle against the moors. There are two important passages in the early chapters of *WH*: Lockwood's being attacked by the dogs and his encounter with the brindled cat, "Grimalkin." In the first *King Lear* is mentioned, and the second refers to *Macbeth*.

B181 Irwin, I. H. "The Home of the Brontës" *The Woman's Journal* ns 15 (Nov 1930) 18–19, 44–46
This is a personal account of a visit to Haworth Parsonage, interwoven with the Brontë story.

B182 Isenberg, David R. "A Gondal Fragment" *BST* 14 (1962) 24–26
This is the description and investigation of a 4½" x 3½" note (reproduced in Plate 4 of the issue) in EB's hand listing the heights and characteristics of Gondal characters. The young Gondal characters are compared with characters in *WH*.

B183 Johnston, Myrtle "The Brontës in Ireland" *Cornhill Magazine* 158 (July 1938) 76–87
The article refers to incidents recorded in William Wright's book, *The Brontës in Ireland* [1893], about the brothers of Patrick Brontë who lived in Ireland.

B184 [Jones, Joseph] "Rare Book Collections. I" *Library Chronicle of the University of Texas* 3 (Spring 1950) 224–225

Brontëana which is "a storehouse of secondary source material" was received by the University of Texas in September 1949. It was accumulated by Alex Symington in association with Thomas J. Wise.

B185 Jordan, John E. "The Ironic Vision of Emily Brontë" *NCF* 20 (June 1965) 1–18

Lockwood is "the city slicker in the haunted house." Opposed to David Cecil's view (see A22) that EB was innocent of irony, Jordan sees in *WH* "a fabric of ironies." Young Catherine, Nelly Dean, and Lockwood are major instruments of EB's irony — through their comments and narrations. The ultimate achievements of both Catherines are additional ironies. The significance of Zillah is discussed and the bird imagery pointed out.

B186 Justus, James "Beyond Gothicism: *Wuthering Heights* and an American Tradition" *Tennessee Studies in Literature* 5 (1960) 25–33

This is an investigation of the elements in *WH* "that make it vital in man's experience." *WH* is compared with the work of Hawthorne, Melville, Dreiser, and Faulkner.

B187 Kellett, E. E. "New Light on the Brontës" *London Quarterly and Holborn Review* 160 (Oct 1935) 591–521

Of all the Brontës, EB was especially influenced by the Methodism in Yorkshire.

B188 Kelly, Charlotte M. "What I Saw at Haworth" *Irish Digest* 78 (Oct 1963) 83–85

A personal description of the interior of the Brontë Museum at Haworth.

B189 Kenton, Edna "Forgotten Creator of Ghosts; Joseph Sheridan Le Fanu, Possible Inspirer of the Brontës" *Bookman* (New York) 69 (July 1929) 528–534 [531–532]

The similarities between *The Purcell Papers* of Le Fanu and the Brontë novels are delineated. It was perhaps from Le Fanu's "occult" writings that EB derived Heathcliff. The tales were "Irish" or "ghostly."

B190 Kite, J. E. [Letter to the Editor] *"Wuthering Heights"* TLS (Mar 16 1951) 165

He has a first edition of *WH* with penciled corrections in what Thomas J. Wise has identified as EB's handwriting. However, Charlotte Brontë did not make use of these corrections in subsequent editions.

B191 Klingopulos, G. D. "The Novel as Dramatic Poem (II): *Wuthering Heights*" *Scrutiny* 14 (Sept 1947) 269–286

Two factors may explain a reader's dislike of *WH*: (1) *WH* is not a moral tale; nor is it a perfect work of art; (2) some of the passages are too insistent and deliberate. The tensions and conflicts in the novel are discussed. EB is "the first writer to have used the novel as a vehicle for that kind of statement which is contained in the finest of English dramatic poetry." *WH* is compared with her poem "Cold in the Earth," and is comparable to *Macbeth* although it does not have that play's coherence.

B191a Kolb, Eduard "An Exercise in Dialect Detection" *Transactions of the Yorkshire Dialect Society* 11 (1955) 11–17

Using excerpts from Joseph's speech in *WH*, the author demonstrates that dialect can be geographically placed by a process of elimination employing the lexical, morphological, and phonological features of dialect.

B192 Lane, Margaret "The Drug-like Brontë Dream" *BST* 12 (1952) 79–87

The four Brontës escaped into a dream world which they had created as children, and each had his own manifestation of it. Charlotte Brontë broke out of it, but EB remained steadfastly in it and through this means achieved her novel and poems.

B192a —— "Emily Brontë in a Cold Climate" *BST* 15 (1968) 187–200
EB does not attempt to humanize the natural world in *WH*; she knew that Nature is alien to Man, even when it is being kind. This modern discussion of *WH* considers some of the criticism the novel has attracted, settings in *WH*, the Gondal story, the characters, the poetic prose, and several smaller points such as the books in *WH* and the number of deaths in *WH*.

B193 —— "French Essays by Charlotte and Emily" *BST* 12 (1954) 273–285
On p 280–285 one essay by EB entitled "The Palace of Death" is translated by the author with the French printed on the opposite page. (See A152, B15, and B81 for other French essays.)

B194 —— "The Palace of Death" *The Listener* 52 (Nov 11 1954) 803–804
This is a translation of EB's devoir "The Palace of Death," written for M Heger on October 18 1842, and a discussion of it, concluding that it is "macabre." The theme is supposed to have been EB's own choice. The author claims that EB saw civilization as a destructive force, and intemperance as the "Viceroy of Death." (See B227 for a criticism of this interpretation. For other French essays see A152, B15, and B81.)

B195 Langman, F. H. "*Wuthering Heights*" *Essays in Criticism* 15 (July 1965) 294–312
The author attempts to "nail down some common faults in the criticism of this novel." The critics fall short on "the significance of the prose style and narrative method, the nature of the love between Catherine and Heathcliff, and the pervasive violence and cruelty." This is an excellent essay which should be read by anyone beginning work on *WH*. Reprinted: A53.

B196 Law, Alice "Branwell Brontë's Novel" *The Bookman* (London) 68 (Apr 1925) 4–6
The evidence is presented for Branwell Brontë's authorship of *WH*.

B197 Lemon, Charles [Letter to the Editor] "Emily Brontë's Missing Novel" *TLS* (Mar 17 1966) 223
This letter is in reply to Letter to the Editor, B167. Hewish did not quote the full Newby letter (Newby refers to *WH* earlier in the letter). Nevertheless, it must be admitted that Newby's carelessness may be the only answer to the problem. Reprinted: B198.

B198 —— "Emily Brontë's Second Novel" *BST* 15 (1966) 29
This is a reprinting of Item B197.

B199 —— "Sickness and Health in *Wuthering Heights*" *BST* 14 (1963) 23–25
The brief lives of the characters in *WH* and their many illnesses "would not have appeared unusual to Emily" because of her own experience with brief life and illness in the Brontë family.

B200 Leslie, Shane "A Brontë Relic" *Time and Tide* 40 (June 13 1959) 683–684
A defense of Cowan Bridge School's reputation is contained in the account by the Reverend Benjamin Allen, of Philadelphia, of his visit there in 1828.

B201 Levin, Harry "Janes and Emilies, Or the Novelist as Heroine" *Southern Review* (Baton Rouge, La) n s 1 (Oct 1965) 735–753
EB is mentioned on p 742–744. This article is concerned with the feminine sex versus the masculine sex, as authors.

B202 Lewis, C. Day "The Poetry of Emily Brontë: A Passion for Freedom" *BST* 13 (1957) 83–99
EB's poetry is related to *WH* and to her religious upbringing. Because of her struggle for freedom, the Gondal poems are full of prisoners and exiles. EB's morality in the poems and *WH* is discussed.

B203 Littell, Philip "Books and Things" *New Republic* 16 (Aug 31 1918) 142
In a discussion of Emily and Charlotte Brontë, Littell says that inaccessibility to facts about EB has augmented her fame.

B204 Livermore, Ann Lapraik "Byron and Emily Brontë" *Quarterly Review* 300 (July 1962) 337–344

WH is seen as a rewriting of Byron's *The Dream.* Heathcliff is Byron, Isabella is Byron's wife, and Catherine Earnshaw is Byron's half-sister. EB's poetry also was influenced by Byron.

B205 Longbottom, John "*Wuthering Heights* and Patrick Branwell **Brontë**" *Yorkshire Notes and Queries* 1 (Feb 1905) 342–346

The author believes that Branwell Brontë was the real author of *WH* and supports his belief with a number of quotes he calls "Biographical Notes."

B206 Lord, Walter F. "The Brontë Novels" *Nineteenth Century* 53 (Mar 1903) 484–495

This article contains criticisms of all the Brontë novels, and "one yawns over *Wuthering Heights.*" EB is not a great artist, but *Agnes Grey* by Anne Brontë "makes a great impression."

B207 MacCarthy, B. G. "Emily Brontë" *Studies: An Irish Quarterly Review* 39 (Mar 1950) 15–30

The story of the Brontës is told with careful adherence to the facts, centering upon EB and emphasizing environmental factors in her life. EB is defined as a "poet-mystic of the natural order," and is shown to reveal her feelings through her poetry.

B208 MacCarthy, Desmond "The Brontës in Their Books" *BST* 10 (1945) 263–264

Any study of Brontë work should exclude a consideration of Brontë biography. EB is proof of the point because "there is an enormous gap which not only no records, but really no plausible conjecture can bridge."

B209 McCaughey, G. S. "An Approach to *Wuthering Heights*" *Humanities Association Bulletin* 15 (Autumn 1964) 28–34

This is an original essay which investigates *WH* from only one viewpoint: the trial of the Earnshaw family. As Hindley weakens over liquor, Catherine weakens over the Linton family, but at the end of the novel, an Earnshaw is master of Wuthering Heights.

B210 McCurdy, Harold Grier "A Study of the Novels of Charlotte and Emily Brontë as an Expression of Their Personalities" *Journal of Personality* 16 (Dec 1947) 109–152

This is a detailed psychological dissection of *WH* and the four novels of Charlotte Brontë. The characters in all five novels are closely examined and compared. The evaluation of the sisters' personalities, on the basis of this examination, is that "Charlotte Brontë is more defensive, Emily more aggressive." In the second half of the article McCurdy compares biographical information with his earlier inferences from the novels and his hypotheses are seemingly corroborated. Among them, regarding *WH* and EB's personality, *WH* "indicated a personality organized at the level of a child's, full of vitality and lacking in conscience, capable of decided alterations between strong aggression and moods of tenderness; and . . . it bespoke great self-absorption and little sociality in the author." The two sisters had a great influence upon each other, and this aspect of their personalities is also investigated.

B211 Mackay, Angus M. "The Brontës: Their Fascination and Genius" *The Bookman* (London) 27 (Oct 1904) 9–17 [14–15]

The author gives the reasons for the public's fascination with the Brontës, and an analysis of Brontë genius.

B212 MacKay, Ruth M. "Irish Heaths and German Cliffs: A Study of the Foreign Sources of *Wuthering Heights*" *Brigham Young University Studies* 7 (Autumn 1965) 28–39

Two principal sources for *WH* were the German "Das Majorat" and the Irish "The Bridegroom of Barna." This article shows how EB welded them together in *WH*. EB's source for the love of Catherine and Heathcliff was the love she and Branwell Brontë had for each other.

B213 MacKereth, James A. "The Greatness of Emily Brontë" *BST* 7 (1929) 175–200

EB should not be analyzed or her works interpreted on a psychological level. She has transmitted in *WH* the idea that Man is "vaster than any temporal aspect or consciousness of himself." MacKereth also discusses *WH* in relation to other great literary works.

B214 McKibben, Robert C. "The Image of the Book in *Wuthering Heights*" *NCF* 15 (Sept 1960) 159–169

". . . just as the window figure is primarily identified with the more tempestuous lovers, so the image of the book is the reflection of the stabilizing love of Cathy and Hareton." The article also contains an unusual interpretation of Heathcliff, and connects a French essay written by EB, "The Butterfly," with *WH*. Reprinted: A104.

B215 MacRae, Elizabeth "Brontë Child Manuscripts at Harvard" *Horn Book Magazine* 17 (Mar – Apr 1941) 108–121

These are the manuscripts of Charlotte and Branwell Brontë only.

*B216 Madden, David "Chapter Seventeen of *Wuthering Heights*" *English Record* 17 (Feb 1967) 2–8

"Emily Brontë's *Wuthering Heights* repeats and anticipates in the transition between the two parts of the book. . . . This chapter [17] has more violence than the others . . . , and symbols have special power. . . ." [From an abstract in *Abstracts of English Studies.*]

B217 Madden, William A. "The Search for Forgiveness in Some Nineteenth-Century English Novels" *Comparative Literature Studies* 3 (1966) 139–153

In *WH* forgiveness is a central theme, as evidenced by Jabes Branderham's sermon. It is a "detached double parable of vengeance, hate, isolation, and death, on the one hand, and forgiveness, love, integration, and life on the other hand. . . ." The novel's message is that the only unforgivable sin is the refusal to forgive. The other novels discussed are *Vanity Fair, Heart of Midlothian, Pilgrim's Progress, Middlemarch, Tess of the D'Urbervilles,* and *Lord Jim.*

B218 Malham-Dembleby, J. "The Lifting of the Brontë Veil" *Fortnightly Review* 81 (Mar 1907) 489–505

The author alleges that Charlotte Brontë wrote *WH*.

B219 Marchand, Leslie A. "An Addition to the Census of Brontë Manuscripts" *NCF* 4 (June 1949) 81–84

Branwell Brontë's manuscripts and some letters written by Charlotte Brontë have been added to the Rutgers University Library. There is no mention of EB, but all of the collection (from the library of J. Alex Symington) has not yet been catalogued.

B220 —— "The Symington Collection" *Journal of the Rutgers University Library* 12 (Dec 1948) 1–15

Although EB is not mentioned, p 2–3 describe the Brontë manuscripts in the collection, particularly Branwell's. Also mentioned are letters from Ellen Nussey to Charlotte Brontë.

B221 Marks, William Sowell, III "The Novel as Puritan Romance: A Comparative Study of Samuel Richardson, the Brontës, Thomas Hardy, and D. H. Lawrence" *Dissertation Abstracts* 25 (Aug 1964) 1214

The author's purpose is ". . . to define and trace the Puritan ideals of love and marriage" in the English novel from Richardson to Lawrence. He discusses "the Brontës' greater sympathy with the demonic and a corresponding criticism of the society which represses it." There are parallels between *WH* and the songs and prophecies of William Blake.

B222 Marsden, Hilda "The Scenic Background of *Wuthering Heights*" *BST* 13 (1957) 111–130

The Law Hill area, a possible locale of *WH*, is described with map, pictures, and references to the novel.

B223 Marshall, William H. "Hareton Earnshaw: Natural Theology on the Moors" *Victorian Newsletter* 21 (Spring 1962) 14–15

Hareton sees Heathcliff as his deity, yet retains the native intelligence to effect his own regeneration. He is compared with Shakespeare's Caliban, and is like Browning's Caliban implicitly, although Browning allows his Caliban to work out his theological structure.

B224 Mathison, John K. "Nelly Dean and the Power of *Wuthering Heights*" *NCF* 11 (Sept 1956) 106–129

This is an excellent treatment of Nelly Dean as an admirable woman whose point of view the reader must reject. The reader is forced to feel the inadequacy of Nelly's wholesome viewpoint, becomes himself an interpreter and judge, and feels "sympathy with genuine passions, no matter how destructive or violent." Reprinted: A53, A104, A165.

B225 Maugham, W. Somerset "The Ten Best Novels: *Wuthering Heights*" *Atlantic Monthly* 181 (Feb 1948) 89–94

EB's almost morbid shyness and solitude are responsible for the method of narration in *WH*. "She hid herself behind a double mask," because she herself was Catherine Earnshaw and Heathcliff. "I think it gave her a thrill of release when she bullied, reviled, and browbeat." Reprinted: A120, A121, A122.

B226 Maurer, K. W. "The Poetry of Emily Brontë" *Anglia* 61 (1937) 442–448

Branwell Brontë was "particularly important in connection with Emily" because she was the one most devoted to him. Her poetry is seen as barely escaping "insipidity and flatness" because of the feeling in it of intense suffering, which is attributed to her involvement in Branwell's tragic life.

B227 Maxwell, J. C. "Emily Brontë's 'The Palace of Death'" *BST* 15 (1967) 139–140

The essay is compared with the devoir of the same title written by Charlotte Brontë. The author disagrees with Margaret Lane's interpretation (B194).

B228 —— "A Shakespearean Comma in *Wuthering Heights*" *The Trollopian* 3 (Mar 1949) 315

This is a short textual note to the effect that the comma was commonly used for emphasis in the nineteenth century. The *WH* example given here is, "Are you, Linton?" The sense is, "Are *you* Linton?" This is young Catherine Linton's question when she first sees Linton Heathcliff.

B228a Mayne, Isobel "Emily Brontë's Mr. Lockwood" *BST* 15 (1968) 207–213

Lockwood is important to the structure of *WH*, and also is a "skilful and realistic technical device by which Emily Brontë communicates with her readers."

B228b Meier, T. K. "*Wuthering Heights* and Violation of Class" *BST* 15 (1968) 233–236

Heathcliff, Nelly Dean, and Joseph are the three characters who upset traditional class lines in *WH*. Moral decline accompanies class violation, and Linton Heathcliff is central to several aspects of the decay.

B229 Melton, James "The Brontë Parsonage Museum" *The Connoisseur* 135 (Apr 1955) 106–107

The Brontë Museum and some of the furniture and portraits are described and illustrated.

B230 Mew, Charlotte M. "The Poems of Emily Brontë" *Temple Bar* 130 (July 1904) 153–167

Primarily EB's poems, but also *WH*, are viewed as preamble to what she might have done had she lived. Her reputation "as a great artist and a repulsive woman" has been built upon *WH*, but the real EB is discoverable in her poems: ". . . sweeter and lighter fancies peer like stars between the masses of dark cloud. . . ." This is a full and appreciative investigation of the poems.

B231 Meyerstein, E. H. W. [Letter to the Editor] "A Brontë Metre" *TLS* (Nov 12 1938) 725–726
The similarity of metre in EB's "No Coward Soul Is Mine" and Felicia Heman's "The Hour of Death" (1824) is pointed out. (See B156 for another comparison of metre.)

B232 Meynell, Alice "Charlotte and Emily Brontë" *Dublin Review* 148 (Apr 1911) 230–243
This is a reprinting of Item A124.

B233 —— "Charlotte and Emily Brontë" *Living Age* 269 (May 27 1911) 515–522
This is a reprinting of Item A124.

B234 Michell, Humfrey "Haworth" *Dalhousie Review* 31 (Summer 1951) 135–141
This is a personal and maudlin account of a visit to Haworth with a description of the town and the Brontë Museum.

B235 Midgley, Wilson "Sunshine on Haworth Moor" *BST* 11 (1950) 309–326
This review of the Brontë history and genius is by a fellow Yorkshireman. The Brontës are briefly compared with Dorothy Wordsworth and Joan of Arc. There is some conjecture, but also some interesting material about Yorkshire custom and reserve, e.g., "Even Nelly Dean only once kissed one of her charges."

B236 Mirsky, Prince D. S. "Emily Brontë" *London Mercury* 7 (Jan 1923) 266–272
Charlotte and Emily Brontë are contrasted as to personality traits and first novels. *WH* is discussed with emphasis upon the characters, briefly compared with other European novels, and pronounced unique (with the possible exception of *Crime and Punishment*) in combining "in the same degree the two qualities of spiritual intensity and artistic efficiency."

B237 —— "Through Foreign Eyes" *BST* 6 (1923) 147–152
EB is viewed subjectively through the author's "foreign eyes." There is an interesting comparison of Rochester and Heathcliff as they were conceived by their creators. EB and Heathcliff are both "outside nature," and EB's art is Latin and French because it is "of conscious and disciplined will." Reprinted: A1.

B238 Moody, Philippa "The Challenge to Maturity in *Wuthering Heights*" *Melbourne Critical Review* 5 (1962) 27–39
This is a perceptive and thorough investigation of the central experience of *WH*, which is the love of Catherine and Heathcliff, accompanied by a discussion of the credibility of *WH* to the reader and the value of the intense emotion in it. The two narrators are also discussed briefly.

B239 Moore, Charles L. "Another Literary Mare's-nest" *The Dial* 53 (Oct 16 1912) 277–278
Leyland, who said Branwell Brontë wrote *WH*, and Malham-Dembleby, who said Charlotte Brontë wrote *WH*, are both proved wrong, with special attention to Malham-Dembleby. Emily and Charlotte Brontë differ in their poetry, their style, and their characters.

B240 Moore-Smith, Prof C. "Brontës in Thornton" *The Bookman* (London) 27 (Oct 1904) 18–22
The author's grandmother was acquainted with Patrick and Maria Brontë when they lived at Thornton.

B241 Moore, T. Sturge "Beyond East and West: A Re-interpretation of Emily Brontë" *Asiatic Review* 37 (Oct 1941) 810–816
EB is discussed from an Eastern point of view, with special attention to her poetry. She is compared with William Blake.

*B242 Morgan, Charles "Emily Brontë" *TLS* [pre 1932]
This is an objective discussion of EB's work. We have very few pieces of autobiographical data on EB, and they did not reveal her inner self. The author briefly reviews the conjectural literature written about her. EB's life was on two planes: the one that Charlotte Brontë and Mrs Gaskell knew, and the mystic. An investigation of her poetry and *WH* reveal that EB was her mystic self in these. Reprinted: A129, A130.

B243 Morgan, Edwin "Women and Poetry" *Cambridge Journal* 3 (Aug 1950) 643–673 [648–656]
The article contains a thorough analysis of EB's poetry, along with a discussion of the poetry of Katherine Philips and Mrs Browning. EB is said to be the greatest of all women poets because she was not influenced by any literary world and her physical isolation allowed her to concentrate on her inner world. The Gondal saga as it relates to her poetry is also discussed.

—— *see* B164.

B244 Moser, Thomas "What Is the Matter with Emily Jane? Conflicting Impulses in *Wuthering Heights*" *NCF* 17 (June 1962) 1–19
The author agrees with "the nineteenth-century view of *Wuthering Heights* as a powerful and imperfect book." He interprets it in a Freudian manner, and some of the Freudian aspects are very well-developed and supported. Reprinted: A131.

Mott, Joan *see* B58 and B59.

B245 Nelson, Jane Gray "First American Reviews of the Works of Charlotte, Emily, and Anne Brontë" *BST* 14 (1964) 39–44
The first American reviews of the novels and the poems "varied . . . from disgust to perplexed enthusiasm." Ten magazines are quoted.

B246 Nelson, Lowry, Jr "Night Thoughts on the Gothic Novel" *Yale Review* 52 (Dec 1962) 236–257
WH is discussed on p 251–256. Heathcliff was an heir to the Gothic hero. *WH* is compared with *Moby Dick* and *Frankenstein*. All three novels are "without either God or devil."

*B247 Nicoll, W. Robertson "Emily Brontë" *British Weekly* (Oct 1908)

B248 Nixon, Ingeborg "The Brontë Portraits: Some Old Problems and a New Discovery" *BST* 13 (1958) 232–238
The "pillar group" portrait of the three Brontë sisters "originally contained a fourth figure, almost certainly that of Branwell himself."

B249 —— "A Note on the Pattern of *Wuthering Heights*" *English Studies* 45 (Supplement 1964) 235–242
This is one of the more thorough analyses of the structure of *WH*. The author points out that the action is "grouped round certain lyrical and dramatic passages. . . ."

B250 O'Byrne, Cathal "The Gaelic Source of the Brontë Genius" *The Columbia* 10 (July 1931) 12–13, 36
The story is told of the marriage of EB's paternal grandparents, with emphasis upon the Irish traits of the Brontë sisters. Hugh Prunty, their grandfather, was famous as a "shanachie" or story-teller. The author also discusses Catholicism in the family. Reprinted: A139.

B251 Odom, Keith Conrad "The Brontës and Romantic Views of Personality" *Dissertation Abstracts* 22 (Dec 1961) 2004–2005
Charlotte, Emily, and Anne Brontë are treated together in an investigation of the degree to which the Brontës employed views of personality held in the English Romantic period. The Romantic view is particularly seen in their attitudes toward childhood. Also Romantic is the fact that their good characters refer to the unity of Nature.

B252 Offor, Richard "The Brontës — Their Relation to the History and Politics of Their Time" *BST* 10 (1943) 150–160
The focus is upon Charlotte Brontë because of "the paucity of evidence" for Emily and Anne. However, this is an interesting account of historical events and trends during the lifetime of the Brontës.

B253 Olsen, Thomas [Letter to the Editor] "The Brontës and Methodism" *TLS* (May 27 1949) 347
This is a contradiction of the idea that EB was steeped in Methodism. (See B157 for a reply.)

B254 Oram, Eanne "Brief for Miss Branwell" *BST* 14 (1964) 28–38
The biographers' comments on the Brontës' aunt, Elizabeth Branwell, and her influence upon the Brontë children have been perhaps unfair. Her contributions, religious and otherwise, are here more favorably evaluated.

B255 —— "Emily and F. D. Maurice: Some Parallels of Thought" *BST* 13 (1957) 131–140
A comparison of Maurice's ideas to the philosophy in *WH* and EB's poetry.

B256 Overton, Grant "Do You Remember?" *Mentor* 17 (Dec 1929) 47–48
This is a brief retelling of the story of *WH* for popular consumption, with a few highlights of EB's family history. Neither is altogether correct.

B257 P.-G., M. E. "Tours Through Literary England: Through the Brontë Country" *Saturday Review* (London) 150 (Sept 13 1930) 310
The Brontë family's life story is told briefly in the context of the Yorkshire country, with map and descriptions.

B258 Parkinson, E. M. "The Brontës' Domestic Servant Problem" *Saturday Review* (London) 150 (Aug 16 1930) 196–197
Both Charlotte and Emily Brontë "had no mercy on their servants." To support this theory, Nelly Dean in *WH* is given as an example: she is made to be lady's maid, nurse, housekeeper, fruit-picker, companion, and seamstress.

B259 Parrish, M. L. "Adventures in Reading and Collecting Victorian Fiction" *Princeton University Library Chronicle* 3 (Feb 1942) 33–44
The author includes the Brontës in his discussion of his career as a book collector. *WH* "is one of the scarcest books in Victorian fiction."

B260 Paul, David "The Novel Art. II." *Twentieth Century* 154 (Oct 1953) 294–301
WH is discussed on p 300–301. *WH* and *Jane Eyre* are compared in the context of EB's and Charlotte Brontë's "wish-fulfillment," a psychological motivation deprecated in the 1930's, but asserted by the author to be essential in any novelist.

B261 Pearsall, Robert Brainard "The Presiding Tropes of Emily Brontë" *College English* 27 (Jan 1966) 267–273
This is a discussion and explication of EB's poetic language in *WH*. The speech of her central characters contains "bold metaphors." EB's "disguise [of misery] was the feverish intellectualization of her tropes. . . . Emily Brontë lusted to expose her troubled soul, and also lusted to cover it up."

*B262 Phelps, William L. "The Mid-Victorians" *The Bookman* [pre 1916]
WH is "more hysterical than historical in its treatment of human nature," but it "has the strength of delirium." EB's personal repression accounts for the passion in *WH*. Reprinted: A143.

B263 Preston, Albert H. "John Greenwood and the Brontës. The Haworth Stationer Throws New Light on Emily" *BST* 12 (1951) 35–38

John Greenwood's notebook relates the doubtful incident of Mr Brontë's giving EB a lesson in marksmanship.

B264 Pritchett, V. S. "Books in General" *New Statesman and Nation* 31 (June 22 1946) 453

This is a modern review of *WH*. The Northern shrewdness and other Northern characteristics are found in the "implacable and belligerent people" in *WH*. Heathcliff's ancestor in literature is Lovelace, "the superb male in full possession of the powers of conspiracy and seduction," but Heathcliff is not so admirable a villain as Lovelace. Reprinted: A53, A104, A194a.

B265 Prunty, Maura "Father of the Brontë Sisters" *Irish Digest* 73 (Dec 1961) 52–54

This short history and character sketch of Patrick Brontë attributes the genius of his daughters principally to their Irish ancestry. "Miss Ellen Nussey . . . was convinced that Emily got some of her facts from her father's narratives."

B266 Quertermous, Harry Maxwell "The Byronic Hero in the Writings of the Brontës" *Dissertation Abstracts* 21 (July 1960) 191–192

The Byronic hero appeared early in the childhood writings of the four Brontës. In EB's work "the Byronic hero, as depicted by the Brontës, reached its greatest realization." Catherine as well as Heathcliff is a Byronic hero; they are both incarcerated, and at the same time divine.

B267 Raine, Kathleen [Emily Brontë's Poems] *New Statesman and Nation* 43 (Mar 8 1952) 277–278. Reply: J. F. Hewish 43 (Mar 29 1952) 375. Rejoinder: 43 (Apr 5 1952) 405

EB is pictured as a woman poet who is unafraid to deal with women as child-murderers and faithless lovers. J. F. Hewish resents this female angle. K. Raine replies, defending her assertion, and says that few women have written poems that would be memorable but for the fact that their authors were women.

B268 Ralli, Augustus "Emily Brontë: The Problem of Personality" *North American Review* 221 (Mar 1925) 495–507

The biography of an author does relate to his work; we can see EB through *WH*. Her characters have a self-consciousness as Shakespeare's characters do, and this makes them psychologically real. Their sarcasm is bound up with EB's nature. She was not at peace with Man, but with Nature; she was a mystic. EB succeeded in depicting the soul and depicting eternity. Reprinted: A146.

B269 Randall, David A. "First American Edition of the Brontës' Poems" *Book Collector* 9 (Summer 1960) 199–201

He comments (in answer to a query in a previous issue, B162) upon the rarity of first editions of the poems, and also mentions first editions of *WH*. (See B23 for another reply.)

B270 Ratchford, Fannie E. "An American Postscript" *BST* 11 (1947) 87–88

The contemporary reading public in America is discussed in relation to *WH* and *Jane Eyre*.

B271 —— [Letter to the Editor] "The Brontës" *TLS* (Dec 11 1948) 697

There are references to the Brontës in letters written by their cousin, Elizabeth Jane Kingston, of Penzance. Among other things, Miss Kingston says that EB should never have written *WH*.

B272 —— "The Brontës' Web of Dreams" *Yale Review* n s 21 (Autumn 1931) 139–157

This is an account of the Brontë childhood plays. EB is discussed on p 154–157, and her poetry is briefly related to the Gondal play.

B273 —— "Correct Text of Emily Brontë's Poems" *BST* 10 (1942) 107–109
This is an appreciative discussion of C. W. Hatfield's (see A80) scholarly textual editing of EB's poems.

B274 —— [Letter to the Editor] "The Gondal Poems" *TLS* (Dec 4 1930) 1041–1042
The author points out some heretofore unknown facts about Gondal which she derived from a study of EB's manuscripts in the Bonnell Collection.

B275 —— "The Significance of the Diary Paper" *BST* 12 (1951) 16–17
This diary paper is the second, in point of date, of four such pieces. Most significant in it is EB's statement that she is writing Augustus Almeda's life.

B276 —— "War in Gondal: Emily Brontë's Last Poem" *The Trollopian* 2 (Dec 1947) 137–155
EB's accounts of war in Gondal, in her poems, reflect her hatred of war with "vivid gory imagery."

B277 Read, Herbert "Charlotte and Emily Brontë" *Yale Review* n s 14 (July 1925) 720–738
This psychological view of the genius of both sisters considers their heredity, environment, possible childhood influences, and education in relation to their works. M Heger was not merely a schoolmaster, but "a master of the art of writing." *WH* has a "spirit of Romanticism" and at the same time it is a novel that reaches "the dignity of classical tragedy" in its evocation of pity and terror. Reprinted: A157, A158, A159.

B278 Reilly, A. J. "Celtic Elements in the Brontë Genius" *Ave Maria* 38 (Sept 23–30 1933) 393–396
One of the Brontë ancestors was the famous Gaelic poet, Padraic O'Prunta. ". . . a more rational explanation" of the Brontë genius is their Celtic heritage. Elements in this heritage are a duality of "aptitude at fighting and their subtle speech," a duality of orderly practicality and imagination, and an intense love of nature. EB's poetry follows the Irish mode rather than the English, and her highly-praised English in *WH* has the "colloquial directness found in English as it is spoken in Ireland."

B279 Reilly, Joseph J. "Some Victorian Reputations" *Catholic World* 145 (Apr 1937) 16–23
WH is discussed on p 20–22. Victorian writers are emerging now from the reactions of their age, and the author reviews EB's literary reputation from the 1850's to 1925 considering both *WH* and her poetry.

B280 Reynolds, Thomas "Division and Unity in *Wuthering Heights*" *University Review* (Kansas City, Mo) 32 (Autumn 1965) 31–37
This is an illuminating and coherent essay. The analogies, balances, and counterpointing in *WH* show the existence of love in hate and hate in love. Alienation leads to fusion, and annihilation to creation.

B281 Rhodes, Margaret G. "A Brief Interlude . . . The Brontës at Silverdale" *BST* 14 (1964) 44–45
Charlotte and Emily Brontë spent one night in Silverdale in 1825 on a holiday from Cowan Bridge School. This is a description of the area and Cove House where they stayed.

B282 Rhys, Ernest "The Haworth Tradition" *BST* 6 (1922) 88–96
"The power of the place [is] behind the power of the book," the author says of *WH*. The universality of *WH* is due to a selection of language that made it real. Reprinted: A1.

B283 Robertson, Charles G. "The Brontës' 'Experience of Life'" *BST* 9 (1936) 37–47

The question of whether or not the Brontë literature should be studied with biographical data in mind is considered. Knowing an author's biography can be misleading, as the author shows by a review of Brontë criticism. *WH* was not as popular eighty years ago as it is now because of the Victorian point of view.

B283a Rosenfield, Claire "The Shadow Within: The Conscious and Unconscious Use of the Double" *Daedalus* 92 (Spring 1963) 326–344

WH is one of the novels, in nineteenth- and twentieth-century fiction, illustrating the use of the double personality. Catherine and Heathcliff are doubles; they differ in sex alone and each possesses a complementary self in his choice of a mate. Only in the world of childhood or death, where the capacity for freedom is infinite, can they exist.

B283b Roseveare, Austin "The Poetry of Emily Brontë" *Poetry Review* (London) 9 (Sept – Oct 1918) 257–267

The sentences in EB's poetry "lead one's thoughts literally towards infinity," yet her poetry is strikingly natural. Roseveare relates her poetry to many of the common human emotions, briefly compares it to Swinburne's, and discusses both form and content.

B284 Rowe, J. Hambley "The Maternal Relatives of the Brontës" *BST* 6 (1923) 135–146

The Branwell family tree, from 1605, is recorded here and includes the possible origin of EB's middle name.

B285 Ruff, William "First American Editions of the Brontë Novels: A Complete Bibliography" *BST* 8 (1934) 143–150

This is a brief account of the publication of the Brontë novels in America with a thorough descriptive bibliography.

B286 Sadleir, Michael "An Addendum to 'Enemies of Books'" *New Colophon* 1 (July 1948) 235–238

The article contains a short discussion of Thomas Cautley Newby, the first publisher of *WH*, and his handling of the publication of *WH*.

*B287 Samaan, Angele Botros "Themes of Emily Brontë's Poetry" in Magdi Wahba, ed *Cairo Studies in English* (1959) 118–134

The author "considers some themes in Emily Brontë's poems: whether they are Gondal or personal poems, 'there is a general feeling of desolation, loneliness, darkness, and gloom.'" [From an abstract in *The Year's Work in English Studies.*]

B288 San Garde, W. A. S. [Letter to the Editor] "The Miraculous Parsonage" *TLS* (Aug 21 1948) 471

W. L. Andrews' (see B29) view of the earlier unpopularity of the Brontë novels is opposed by this writer, who remembers his mother's saying that the Brontë novels were "all the go."

B288a Schmidt, Emily Tresselt "From Highland to Lowland: Charlotte Brontë's Editorial Changes in Emily's Poems" *BST* 15 (1968) 221–226

Charlotte Brontë made changes in EB's poems in 1846 with her approval. In 1850, after EB's death, Charlotte made changes in another group of Emily's poems. The 1850 alterations are compared with those made in 1846, and found to be more extensive.

B289 Scholfield, B. [Letter to the Editor] "The Haworth Moors" *Spectator* 190 (May 22 1953) 678

The writer disagrees with J. Hawkes (see B161): ". . . let the moorland stand for light." He also points out the modernity of Haworth when the Brontës lived there; e.g., they had a daily newspaper and a train to London. (See B28 for a reply.)

B290 Schorer, Mark "Fiction and the Matrix of Analogy" *Kenyon Review* 11 (Autumn 1949) 539–560

The "matrix of analogy" is "that whole habit of value association." The novels treated are *Persuasion, WH,* and *Middlemarch. WH* is discussed on p 544–550. The novel is no tragedy; it is a "moral teething" for EB as well as for Heathcliff. The essay contains an explication of the animal imagery in *WH,* and considers the verbs, metaphors, and epithets used. Reprinted: A165, A167, A194a; partial reprinting: A139a.

B291 —— "Technique as Discovery" *Hudson Review* 1 (Spring 1948) 67–87

WH has a "theme of the moral magnificence of unmoral passion," a theme impossible to sustain. Two aspects of EB's technique, however, objectify it: (1) Her narrative perspective has the two elements, conventional emotion (Lockwood) and conventional morality (Nelly Dean). (2) The perspective operates over a long period of time. Reprinted: A167.

B291a Schreiner, Wilhelmina R. "The Criticism of Emily Brontë" *University of Pittsburgh: Bulletin of MA Theses* 34 (1937) 422

Criticisms of *WH* and EB's poems, examined from the time EB's work was originally published, show something of the literary temper of the times and of the personality of the critic.

B292 Seccombe, Thomas "Place of the Brontës among Women Novelists of the Last Century" *BST* 5 (Apr 1913) 8–12

The title is a misnomer; the article discusses Charlotte Brontë only.

B293 Shannon, Edgar F., Jr "Lockwood's Dreams and the Exegesis of *Wuthering Heights*" *NCF* 14 (Sept 1959) 95–109

Ruth Adams (see B22) asserts Branderham's sermon text to be Genesis 4; instead, it is Matthew 18. The author also repudiates Dorothy Van Ghent's dream interpretation. The thematic problem of the novel is the nature of Catherine's offense. In regard to Heathcliff: "In the terms of Emily Brontë's moral equation, there is no autonomous evil in the universe." Hate is a corollary of love, and "evil derives solely from separation — from the denial of sympathy and love." (See also B39). Reprinted: A104, A194a.

*B293a Smith, David "The Panelled Bed and the Unrepressible Wish of *Wuthering Heights*" *Paunch* 30 (1967) 40–47

B293b Smith, David J. "The Arrested Heart: Familial Love and Psychic Conflict in Five Mid-Victorian Novels" *Dissertation Abstracts* 27 (1966) 1839A

The hypothesis of the dissertation is that principal characters in each of the novels (*Jane Eyre, The Mill on the Floss, Wuthering Heights, Pendennis,* and *The History of Henry Esmond*) are motivated by an unconscious mental conflict between an incest wish and an incest taboo. The conflict explains many aspects of the characters' inner and outer lives; it also illuminates the structure and the meaning of the novels.

B294 Snowden, Keighley "The Brontës as Artists and as Prophets" *BST* 4 (Mar 1909) 78–92

This is a discussion of past and contemporary criticism of the novels of Charlotte and Emily Brontë.

B295 —— "The Enigma of Emily Brontë" *Fortnightly Review* 124 (Aug 1928) 195–202

WH was written by a woman who had felt love, passion, and pain. Two sources for *WH* are suggested: Ruysbroeck's *The Heavenly Espousals* and EB's possible romantic attachment to the curate William Weightman. Three of her poems are connected with Weightman.

B296 Solomon, Eric "The Incest Theme in *Wuthering Heights*" *NCF* 14 (June 1959) 80–83

There is internal evidence in *WH* that Catherine and Heathcliff could possibly be half-brother and -sister. If the novel is read with this possibility in mind, the tragedy would be

greater, the emotion heightened, and the inevitable separation of the two lovers more logical.
Reprinted: A104, A194a.

B297 Spark, Muriel "The Brontës As Teachers" *New Yorker* 41 (Jan 22 1966)
    30–33
    All four Brontës disliked teaching, but EB was the only one "to get out of the predicament
with all speed."

B298 Stedman, Jane W. "The Genesis of the Genii" *BST* 14 (1965) 16–19
    The young Brontës based their Genii to a greater extent on *Tales of the Genii* by James
Ridley than on *Arabian Nights*.

*B299 Stollard, M. L. "The Brontës and Their Visits to Leeds" *Yorkshire Evening
    Post* (May 7 1919)

B300 —— "The Brontës in Leeds" *BST* 13 (1959) 360–362
    Leeds was the Brontës' shopping center. At Leeds Mr Brontë bought the famous wooden
soldiers that began the plays, and "the children were . . . brought up on Leeds newspapers."

B301 Strachan, Pearl "Across the Moors" *Christian Science Monitor* (May 24
    1947) 10
    This article describes a personal walk across the moors and tells the Brontë story. The moors
were the most powerful environmental influence on the works of the Brontës.

B302 Sutcliffe, Halliwell "The Spirit of the Moors" *BST* 2 (Jan 1903) 174–190
    "The outer world knew nothing of the storm and fret of Haworth Moor till *Wuthering
Heights* was born." The characters in *WH* would not live without their surroundings.

*B303 Symons, Arthur "Emily Brontë" *The Nation* 23 (Aug 24 1918) 546–547
    WH is called "one long outcry" from a woman who possessed "passion without sensuous-
ness." The novel is praised for "the mystery of its terror," but it is not well-constructed. Further-
more, "her narrative is dominated by sheer chance and guided by mere accident." Reprinted:
A186, B304.

B304 —— "Emily Brontë" *Living Age* 299 (Oct 12 1918) 119–121
    This is a reprinting of Item B303.

*B305 T., M. "The Brontës of Haworth" *Public Library Journal* 5 (1932)

B306 Taylor, Robert H. "The Singular Anomalies" *Princeton University Library
    Chronicle* 17 (Winter 1956) 71–76
    This is a discussion of the Parrish Collection at Princeton University which contains early
editions of *WH* and *Poems by Currer, Ellis, and Acton Bell*.

B307 Thompson, Wade "Infanticide and Sadism in *Wuthering Heights*" *PMLA*
    78 (Mar 1963) 69–74
    This is ". . . an interpretation of *Wuthering Heights* based upon the extraordinary sadism
which underlies Emily Brontë's concept of emotional relationships. . . ." Reprinted: A53; partially reprinted: A139a.

B308 Thorburn, Donald B. "The Effects of the Wesleyan Movement on the Brontë
    Sisters, as Evidenced by an Examination of Certain of Their Novels" *Microfilm
    Abstracts* 8 (1948) 109–111
    Methodism affected the Brontës both consciously and unconsciously, and it is reflected in
their "attitude toward liquor, toward dress, their anti-Catholic feeling, their sabbatarianism,
their anti-High Church feeling, their attitude toward the sanctity of daily work . . . their use
of the Bible for quotation and daily guidance, their humanitarianism, their belief in the worth
of the common man, their belief in salvation through free choice, and their enthusiasm for the
Evangelical type of religion and for missionary work." Their novels prove that they were
"spiritual children of Methodism."

B309 Tinker, Chauncey Brewster "Poetry of the Brontës" *Saturday Review of Literature* 1 (Jan 10 1925) 441–442
This is a thorough analysis of EB's poetry. In spite of all the Brontë biography "the day will come . . . when . . . the literary work of the three sisters [will be] judged on its merits and not merely prized for the light it throws on their biography." All the Brontës lack discipline in their poetry; EB can "strike a false note," but she is the poetic genius of the family. There is "unchastened emotionalism," an "emphasis on freedom" and "intense self-confidence" in her poetry. Reprinted: A189.

B310 Tompkins, J. M. S. "Caroline Helstone's Eyes" *BST* 14 (1961) 18–28
The heroine of *Shirley* by Charlotte Brontë was, according to Charlotte, modeled on EB. This article discusses the likelihood of Caroline in the novel being modeled on Anne Brontë and discusses the relationship of the three Brontë sisters.

B311 Traversi, Derek "*Wuthering Heights* after a Hundred Years" *Dublin Review* 222 (Spring 1949) 154–168
EB's models for *WH* may have been romantic melodramas, and *WH* could be called one too, but after this has been granted we must consider its dramatic intensity, morality, and mysticism. The two themes are the " 'personal' and 'social' aspects [which] stand in the closest relationship to one another." [The second half of this article is similar to the author's essay "The Brontë Sisters and *Wuthering Heights*" (A190).] Partially reprinted: A139a.

B312 Turnell, Martin "*Wuthering Heights*" *Dublin Review* 206 (Jan 1940) 134–149
This is a comprehensive well-supported social analysis which assesses *WH* as "one of the most tremendous indictments of contemporary civilization in the whole of nineteenth-century literature." The novel is a constructive social criticism and the real subject "is a conflict between two profoundly different ways of life. . . ."

B313 Vaisey, The Hon Mr Justice "*Wuthering Heights*: A Note on Its Authorship" *BST* 11 (1946) 14–15
Regarding the theory of Branwell Brontë's part in the production of *WH*: Chapters I, II, III and the early part of Chapter IV differ from the rest of the book. "It is Branwell rather than Mr Lockwood who is speaking."

B314 Van Ghent, Dorothy "The Window Figure and the Two-Children Figure in *Wuthering Heights*" *NCF* 7 (Dec 1952) 189–197
This is an outstanding myth-and-symbol interpretation of *WH*. The Window Figure is well-supported by many instances in the novel. The Two-children Figure, which is related to several of EB's poems, also leads to interesting speculation.

B315 Vaughan, C. E. "Charlotte and Emily Brontë: A Comparison and a Contrast" *BST* 4 (Apr 1912) 217–235
The sisters had in common passion, lyricism, and revolt, but EB was the more intense and Charlotte Brontë had more humor.

B316 Waddington-Feather, John "Emily Brontë's Use of Dialect in *Wuthering Heights*" *BST* 15 (1966) 12–19
EB uses dialect "in comparatively large amounts" on fifteen occasions in *WH*, to "create character and mood." Her representations are quite accurate, though not always consistent. The emphasis in this article is upon EB's artistic use of dialect rather than the dialect itself.

B317 Walbank, Alan [Letter to the Editor] " 'The Visionary' and 'The Eve of St. Agnes' " *TLS* (June 18 1954) 393
EB's poem "The Visionary" and Keats' "The Eve of St. Agnes" are compared, and their similarity in theme and expression is noted.

B318 Ward, Mrs Humphry *"Wuthering Heights"* BST 2 (Jan 1906) 227–232
This is a reprinting of Item A199.

B319 Watson, Melvin R. "Tempest in the Soul: The Theme and Structure of *Wuthering Heights"* NCF 4 (Sept 1949) 87–100
WH is analogous to Elizabethan drama. Heathcliff is "a Hamlet without Hamlet's fatal irresolution," and the novel is structurally organized like a five-act tragedy. The author concludes that *WH* is the product of a mature artist. Reprinted: A104, A201.

B320 —— *"Wuthering Heights* and the Critics" *The Trollopian* 3 (Mar 1949) 243–263
This is an excellent and detailed review of one hundred years of criticism of *WH*. Earlier criticism was, for the most part, derogatory and confused. "Since 1920 more rational, sensible criticism on *Wuthering Heights* has appeared than during the seventy-odd preceding years. . . ." Noted as worst are the parallel school, the autobiographical school, and the Freudian school. J. A. MacKereth and David Cecil (see B213 and A22) are credited with the most competent interpretations. Reprinted: A53.

B321 Weir, Edith M. "Contemporary Reviews of the First Brontë Novels" *BST* 11 (1947) 89–96
The 1848 English reviews are reprinted here.

B322 —— "New Brontë Material Comes to Light; A Picture Attributed to Emily; Letters from the Hegers" *BST* 11 (1949) 249–261
A watercolor is discovered which is supposed to have been painted by EB when she was in Brussels. It is reproduced on the frontispiece of this issue, and is judged by the author to be genuine.

B323 West, Rebecca "The Role of Fantasy in the Work of the Brontës" *BST* 12 (1954) 255–267
The emphasis is upon *WH*, which has a triple significance: it is a novel in which the truth is told about the characters; it is a critical work exposing the English society to which Lockwood belonged; and it is a poetical work because it interprets the universe.

B324 Wilkins, Mary E. "Emily Brontë and *Wuthering Heights"* *Booklover's Magazine* 1 (May 1903) 514–519
EB is evaluated as an author. Although *WH* has "the repulsiveness of power," EB is intent upon the truth, and handles brutality and coarseness "like another woman would a painted fan."

B325 Willis, Irene Cooper "The Authorship of *Wuthering Heights"* *The Trollopian* 2 (Dec 1947) 157–168
The claim that Branwell Brontë wrote *WH* was first made twenty years after the novel was published. Evidence is presented here against the allegations of those who say they were witnesses to events which tend to support Branwell's partial or complete authorship of *WH*.

B326 Willson, Jo Anne A. " 'The Butterfly' and *Wuthering Heights*: A Mystic's Eschatology" *Victorian Newsletter* 33 (Spring 1968) 22–25
This is a good correlation of one of EB's essays with *WH*. "It is the purpose of this paper to suggest that the 'why' of *Wuthering Heights* may be found in one of the five seldom-discussed essays written by Emily Brontë while she was a student at . . . Brussels, in 1842." These essays were EB's first attempts at formulating a philosophy, and the essays, like *WH*, appeal more to perception than to reason. "The Butterfly" is especially a philosophical predecessor of *WH* in its examination of the forces of good and evil, and the reason for evil on earth. EB writes in the essay: ". . . each suffering of our unhappy nature is only a seed for that divine harvest which will be gathered when sin . . . [and] death . . . will leave their former victims to an eternal realm of happiness and glory."

B327 Willy, Margaret "Emily Brontë: Poet and Mystic" *English* 6 (Autumn 1946) 117–122

This is a discussion of EB and her poems. The influences upon EB were the solitude of her life, the stimulus of the Brontë childhood composition, her brother Branwell, and the moors. The author suggests that EB felt a death-wish that struggled with her love of life, and that both impulses are reflected in her poems.

B327a Wilson, Angus "Evil in the English Novel" *Kenyon Review* 29 (Mar 1967) 167–194

WH is briefly discussed on p 181–183 as the author traces "transcendent good and evil" — especially evil — in the English novel. Heathcliff is a fallen angel, a representation coming directly from the Gothic. Even though he is not redeemed by Catherine's love, as Rochester is redeemed by Jane Eyre's, yet their love transcends the rest of the events of the book.

*B328 Wilson, David "Emily Brontë: First of the Moderns" *Modern Quarterly Miscellany* 1 (1947)

B329 Wilson, The Hon Lady "The Brontës as Governesses" *BST* 9 (1939) 217–235

Since very little is known about EB as a governess, the discussion centers upon the other Brontës.

B330 Wood, Butler "Influence of the Moorlands on Charlotte and Emily Brontë" *BST* 6 (1922) 79–87

There was a strong influence of the moorlands on the Brontë character; EB's nature-worship is reflected in *WH*. Reprinted: A1.

B331 —— "Some Bibliographical Notes on the Brontë Literature" *BST* 4 (Mar 1911) 189–198

This article discusses current Brontë biography and some of the events connected with publication of the Brontë novels.

B332 Woodring, Carl "The Narrators of *Wuthering Heights*" *NCF* 11 (Mar 1957) 298–305

The author points out the further value — in addition to those values mentioned by other critics — of Mr Lockwood, the stranger, and Nelly Dean, the intimate. Nelly Dean adds much warmth to the novel without interfering with the actions of the main characters. Reprinted: A104, A165.

B333 Worth, George J. "Emily Brontë's Mr. Lockwood" *NCF* 12 (Mar 1958) 315–320

Lockwood deludes himself (but not the reader) about his own character and personality, which was deliberately drawn by EB not only to act as a foil to Heathcliff, but also to be an ordinary man through which the reader might see and believe the events and people of *WH*. Reprinted: A104.

C Books and Articles in Foreign Languages

C1 Bataille, Georges "Emily Brontë et le mal" *Critique* 13 No 117 (Feb 1957) 99–112

C2 —— *La Littérature et le mal* (Paris: Gallimard 1957)

C3 Bengtsson, Frans S. *Folk som sjöng* (Stockholm: Norstedt 1956)

C4 Bleikasten, André "La Passion dans *Les Hauts de Hurlevent*" *Bulletin de la Faculté des Lettres de Strasbourg* 36 [pre 1958] 357–364

C5 Blondel, Jacques *Emily Brontë: Expérience spirituelle et création poétique* (Paris: Presses Universitaires de France 1956) (See A131 for a partial translation.)

C6 ——— "Emily Brontë: Récentes explorations" *Études anglaises* 11 (Oct – Dec 1958) 323–330

*C7 ——— "Nouveaux regards sur Emily Brontë et *Wuthering Heights*" *Annales de la Faculté des Lettres et Sciences Humaines d'Aix* 1961

*C8 Carrère, Félix "*Les Hauts de Hurlevent* d'Emily Brontë, histoire d'amour?" *Annales de la Faculté des Lettres d'Aix* 32 (1958) 75–89

C9 Dahm, Hildegard "Die Technik der Charakterdarstellung und das Künstlerische Gesamtbild der Charaktere im Roman *Wuthering Heights* von Emily Brontë" Innsbruck 1955 (Dissertation)

C10 Debu-Bridel, Jacques *Le Secret d'Emily Brontë* (Paris: Ferenczi 1950)

C11 Dupont, V. "Trois Notes sur les Brontës" *Études anglaises* 6 (Feb 1953) 1–27

C12 Ellisiv, Steen "Problemet Emily Brontë" *Edda* 49 (1949) 161–178

C13 Escombe, Lucienne *Emily Brontë et ses démons* (Paris and Clermont: Fernand Serlot 1941)

C14 Fréchet, René "Emily Brontë et son élan mystique" *Foi education* 27 (1957) 95–103

C15 Froese, Fritz "Untersuchungen zu Emily Brontë's Roman *Wuthering Heights*" Königsberg 1920 (Dissertation)

C16 Jaloux, Edmond "Le Mystère d'Emily Brontë" *D'Eschyle à Giraudoux* (Librairie universelle de France 1947)

C17 Kuhlmann, Rudolf *Der Natur-Paganismus in der Weltanschauung von Emily Brontë* (Bonn: Schloppe 1926)

C18 Las Vergnas, Raymond "Powys, l'homme tranquille du Dorset" *Revue de Paris* (September 1965) 98–103

C19 Messiaen, P. "Les Hauts-de-Hurle-Vent" *Revue des Cours et Conférences* 40 (1938) 189–192

C20 Ocampo, Victoria *Emily Brontë: (Terra incognita)* (Buenos Aires: Sur 1938)

*C21 Rébora, P. "Emily Brontë" [I Libri del Giorno] (November 1926)

C22 Traz, Robert de *La Famille Brontë* (Paris: A Michel 1938)

C23 ——— "L'Enfance des Brontës" *Revue de Paris* 45 (1938) 579–605

C24 Wells, Augustin *Les Soeurs Brontë et l'étranger* (Paris: Rodstein 1937)

Chronological Index

1900–1909

A20	A112	B5	B140	B218
A40	A138	B6	B143	B230
A64	A161	B10	B151	B240
A69	A169	B11	B166	B247
A87	A171	B14	B177	B294
A96	A186a	B90	B205	B302
A100	A199	B122	B206	B318
A105	A206a	B127	B211	B324

1910–1919

A7	A164	A214	B68	B233
A24	A169a	A216	B69	B239
A26	A170	A222	B83	B262
A47	A172		B134	B283b
A66	A176	B1	B142	B292
A115	A177	B2	B146a	B299
A118	A178	B16	B154	B303
A124	A196	B17	B176	B304
A137	A205	B18	B203	B315
A143	A207	B25	B232	B331

1920–1929

A6	A91	A185	B33	B173
A6a	A94a	A186	B70	B189
A21	A97	A187	B77	B196
A29	A98	A197	B78	B213
A30	A109	A202	B92	B236
A36	A113	A206	B99	B237
A42	A116	A212	B101	B256
A44	A132	A213	B101a	B268
A57	A146	A215	B119	B277
A58	A159	A219	B121	B282
A59	A166	A220	B131	B284
A67	A173	A221	B144	B295
A68	A174		B145	B309
A71	A175	B12	B147	B330
A81	A179	B20	B155	

1930–1939

A5	A78	A162	B103	B231
A8	A93	A198	B109	B242
A9	A94b	A203	B111	B250
A16	A99	A208	B112	B257
A18	A102	A209	B113	B258
A19	A107	A217	B115	B272
A22	A117	A218	B126	B274
A32	A119		B128	B278
A33	A127	B24	B150	B279
A37	A128	B41	B156	B283
A41	A130	B50	B159	B285
A48	A134	B51	B169	B291a
A51	A135	B53	B175	B305
A52	A139	B57	B181	B329
A60	A141	B58	B183	
A73	A154	B59	B187	
A77	A157	B65	B226	

1940–1949

A1	A129	B44	B141	B271
A10	A136	B46	B152	B273
A12	A145	B47	B157	B276
A13	A148	B48	B163	B286
A15a	A150	B52	B164	B288
A25	A152	B67	B174	B290
A39	A153	B71	B178	B291
A61	A156	B72	B180	B301
A70	A189	B73	B191	B308
A74	A195	B76	B208	B311
A76		B81	B210	B312
A80	B3	B95	B215	B313
A82	B7	B96	B219	B319
A83	B13	B98	B220	B320
A84	B29	B100	B225	B321
A101	B30	B104	B228	B322
A108	B31	B110	B241	B325
A110	B32	B114	B252	B327
A120	B36	B116	B253	B328
A122	B37	B117	B259	
A123	B42	B120	B264	
A126	B43	B125	B270	

1950–1959

A3	A142	B22	B135	B229
A4	A144	B27	B136	B234
A11	A149	B28	B137	B235
A17	A155	B34	B138	B243
A23	A158	B35	B148	B248
A28	A160	B45	B153	B255
A34	A163	B55	B160	B260
A40a	A167	B56	B161	B263
A43	A168	B60	B162	B267
A49	A180	B63	B165	B275
A55	A181	B74	B171	B287
A62	A182	B75	B172a	B289
A85	A188	B79	B179	B293
A86	A190	B80	B184	B296
A92	A191	B85	B190	B300
A94	A192	B86	B191a	B306
A95	A194	B87	B192	B314
A103	A200	B88	B193	B317
A111	A211	B93	B194	B323
A114		B105	B200	B332
A121	B8	B107	B202	B333
A126a	B15	B118	B207	
A133	B19	B123	B222	
A140	B21	B132	B224	

1960–1968

A2	A104	B49	B158	B238
A2a	A106	B54	B167	B244
A4a	A125	B61	B168	B245
A14	A131	B62	B170	B246
A15	A139a	B64	B172	B249
A27	A147	B66	B182	B251
A31	A151	B70a	B185	B254
A33a	A165	B82	B186	B261
A35	A183	B82a	B188	B265
A38	A184	B84	B192a	B266
A45	A193	B89	B195	B269
A46	A194a	B91	B197	B280
A48a	A201	B94	B198	B281
A50	A204	B97	B199	B283a
A53	A210	B102	B201	B288a
A54		B105a	B204	B293a
A56	B4	B106	B209	B293b
A60a	B9	B108	B212	B297
A63	B11a	B123a	B214	B298
A65	B19a	B124	B216	B307
A72	B23	B129	B217	B310
A75	B26	B130	B221	B316
A79	B37a	B133	B223	B326
A88	B38	B139	B227	B327a
A89	B39	B146	B228a	
A90	B40	B149	B228b	